What people a

This is a brilliant book. I just wis.. .. ....
my own children were younger!

It is a treasure trove of insight, information and inspiration;
with excellent questions and ideas for deepening the conversations in families, helping them to become rich places for the
exploration of deep values and character formation. Every
parent needs it in hand.

> - **Tim Costello AO,** Former CEO and Chief Advocate,
> World Vision Australia

Raising Kids Who Care couldn't arrive at a better time for ourselves, our kids and our communities.

Our world is riven by individualism, atomisation, disconnection. Global fault lines, conflict, pandemics, breaches in the
social fabric, survivor of the fittest attitudes, consumerism
and Big Tech encroachment into every aspect of our lives,
have led to a breaking of ties that bind, a severing of deeper
connections and mutual care. Empathy is under threat,
eroded by cruelty, bullying, aggression. The natural softness
and kindness in children is being knocked out of them. We
have become numb to suffering.

Susy Lee has done us a service with this easy to read, accessible and practical book. She brings us back to what is important and valuable and to be desired in this life. She explores
how we and our children can care about our inner lives, about
relationships and about our world. Her book offers timely
help on raising emotionally intelligent, ethical, sensitive and
empathetic children who will act for the common good and
make a difference in the world.

> - **Melinda Tankard Reist,** Author, speaker, campaigner

As a twenty-two-year veteran educator and a homeschooling mom, I have not been more excited to recommend a resource for parents in a long time. Raising Kids Who Care is not just a book—it's a tool to help parents have real conversations with their children. In a culture that revolves around technology and consumerism, parents have to be intentional if they want to raise kids who aren't just seeking the world's idea of success but who actually have character and vision for making their community a better place.

Through research, statistics, thought-provoking questions, and springboards for conversation, *Raising Kids Who Care* is a unique approach in the parenting space today that offers practical strategies and hopeful encouragement. If you are a parent who desires to raise kids with character and compassion, this book is a must-have.

- **Jennifer Hayes Yates**, Educator (USA)

This remarkable book is about hope that change is possible. As a caring parent, an inspiring practitioner with a deep sense of social justice, and a brilliant peace scholar, the author invites us on the journey of nurturing hope in the world, one family at a time. I cannot wait to delve into each of the 40 family conversations in this book with my family.

- **Dr Dong Jin Kim**, ISE Senior Research Fellow in Peace and Reconciliation Studies, Trinity College, Dublin

There is a huge secret to life which most families - and most parenting books - completely miss. That we humans are happiest when we are living for each other, and discovering the fun that brings. In a society that is all about 'me' we have never been more stressed or miserable. Caring is a word that holds the key to life going well, and is the real heart of being human. This book shows you how to foster it...

Brightly and clearly written, with real personality, this book turns on its head our focus on making kids happy, and instead shows how to make them generators of happiness. And (as we all know deep down) that's the only lasting happiness there is.

- **Steve Biddulph AM,** Bestselling author of Raising Girls and Raising Boys

Susy Lee invites us to travel alongside our kids, to discover real life ways to build resilience, the capacity to handle conflict, find contentment and make a difference in the world. In an era where our fears for our kid's futures are heightened and we are all too aware of our own inadequacies as parents this book is a word of hopefulness. Its more than just hopes or dreams though – it's an invitation to positive proactive parenting. Grab it with both hands - it's well and truly worth it.

- **Louise Bartlett**, Children & Families Ministry Facilitator, Baptist Churches NSW & ACT

Wise, warm, imaginative and intensely practical … *Raising Kids Who Care* is like a blueprint for building strong families and caring communities. Highly recommended for anyone who cares about the future of our children and our society.

- **Hugh Mackay AO,** Psychologist, social researcher and bestselling author

Our world and most importantly our children are being bombarded in every aspect of their life. As parents and carers an enabling environment to create kids who care has never been harder or more important. Susy Lee's *Raising Kids Who Care* provides a formulaic, data driven approach supported by a workbook for all readers including the kids! Read it and then practice so you and your clan can enable the difference we all yearn for – generational improvement. A must read for those who want to see kids fly, soar, and become butterflies for change.

- **Karen James**, CEO Business for Development, Author and Advocate for Women

I confess to being tired of books of parenting advice. After reading through the usual list of do's and don'ts the only thing most of us can agree on is that we don't make the grade. Susy Lee's approach is different. She offers a way of parenting that feels authentic, achievable and, most importantly, could really make a difference to the world. She offers hope, encouragement and practical wisdom to every hard-pressed and bewildered parent who yearns to speak to their kids about what really matters.

- **Dr Roger Bretherton**, Associate Professor and Clinical Psychologist

More than just a how-to guide, or a parenting manual, *Raising Kids Who Care* offers personal reflections and practical tools to help families rise to the big personal, social and global challenges of our sometimes bewildering times. Each chapter outlines, in a clear and engaging way, a guided conversation for families to use to tackle issues we often avoid or feel overwhelmed by.

Susy Lee writes with humour and disarming honesty and vulnerability about her own personal and parenting journey… Anyone who wants to nurture kind, compassionate, courageous and committed children should read *Raising Kids Who Care*. In fact, anyone who wants to be a kind, compassionate, courageous and committed person who makes a difference in the world should read it.

- **Ben Thurley**, CEO, INF Australia

As a pastor, I see how busy families are as they juggle lots of competing demands. It can be easy to lose sight of what so many parents really want – to raise children who care! Susy Lee has created a fantastic Australian work that curates deep reflective thinking and then uses that research to develop games and conversations that bring families together. I love her passion and honesty. You can tell this is someone who has sought to live this out in her own life and family. I would recommend this book to all the families I know! This is also a valuable resource for churches wanting to engage with the wider community and create more spaces for families to wrestle with the big questions of life in a fun way.

-   **Rev. Christine Redwood**, Pastor

Raising Kids Who Care is a book for the times we are in. Susy Lee takes us on a journey of understanding ourselves and those around us, and she stretches our greater world view. How does she do this? It's a new approach and it's led by the kids.

I have seen many books for parents and many for kids, but very few that tackle the real family conversations that are needed. Framed in the format of a trip, this book is for families to roll up their sleeves and enjoy the journey of discovery together – discovering one another and the amazing world in which we live.

-   **Karen Wilson,** President, Baptist World Alliance Women; CEO Global Leadership Network Australia; Mother and new grandmother!

As I read Susy Lee's book, I am genuinely excited for my son and young parents like him. These parents can now have this powerful resource that is practically structured, extremely accessible, and wonderfully creative. This book will wisely guide them to hold important conversations that are life-giving for their children and their family as a whole.

Cleverly child-focused, the book reinforces the fact that children are not just passive sponges but have voice, and when given the chance to explore all that life is, within the safety of a family relationship, they can flourish and find guidance by having the chance to talk through critical issues that will form their character, guide their choices, and strengthen their mental, relational, and spiritual wellbeing.

What is different about this book is that it does not just articulate the challenges we all experience when thinking about raising children who will become quality people, it actually focuses more on the solution and gently instructs in ways that are about '*good enough*' parenting.

- **Anthony Sell**, Director of Design & Learning, SEED: Growing redemptive changemakers for a rapidly shifting world.

I am stunned by the level of thought Susy Lee has put into this book. It is going to be a treasured title that doesn't sit on the shelves gathering dust but instead turns up on dining tables or kitchen benches, dog-eared and loved. Loved because children will come away feeling heard and appreciated, their opinions sought, and an increased sense of belonging. Loved because adults will burst with pride in response to their children's suggestions and insights.

Additionally, I think this book could become a trusted conversation starter for anyone interested in gathering their children's friends and their families into these discussions. Whether around the BBQ or after preparing a batch of toasted sandwiches, neighbourhoods could come together and be prompted to talk about what matters most.

- **Jo Hood,** CEO, mainly Ministries, (NZ, Aus, UK) Mother of two, mother-in-law to two, grandmother of two.

Not content to let Instagram and Netflix raise our children, Susy Lee has written a brilliant guidebook that helps kids to put down their screens and dive into deep family conversations about critical social issues. If you want your family to care more about others, social justice, the planet, and culture in general, use this book! It's fun, practical, inspiring, and it might just change the world!

- **Michael Frost**, Morling College, Sydney

An incredible way to exchange views and bond as a family. The conversations really helped our family to have important and meaningful conversations about our opinions and world views.

    – **Jayden**, 16

A plethora of versatile, thought-provoking and fun family conversations to promote positive realisations and action.

    – **Alanah**, 14

Raising
KIDS
Who
CARE

**Practical conversations for
exploring stuff that matters, together**

SUSY LEE

To my sons TJ and Josh who give me so much joy.

*I'm very proud of the caring people you've become
and the ways you're contributing to the world.*

*And to Brian - their wonderful role model -
without you I'd have none of this.*

Your love makes everything possible.

*The cover illustration is our boys and the cousins
they grew up with – so much love and fun!*

*The illustrations throughout the book were drawn
by my talented friend Penny Rankin.*

Contents

CONVERSATIONS LIST

For Our Inner Selves:

For Our World:

PREFACE

When I was six months pregnant with my first child, my husband and I moved into a flat with my brother-in-law and his wife. We planned to live together for six months, but it turned into six years with four sons between us! It was a wonderful time. Two of the boys were born four weeks apart, so we bought a twin pram and breastfed on the lounge together as my older toddler entertained us. I only had to cook every second night; we never needed babysitters; and Karen and I would do all our shopping with the kids in the car – one of us would jump out to go into a shop while the other drove around the block. We were so efficient we'd be off to a different playground every day.

This worked because Karen and I made it work. Because we're very different people, it took a while to become a team. I'd worry that Karen thought I was hopeless at housework and cake-making and dress-up costumes. She'd worry that I thought she wasn't up to whatever I was doing (which I, of course, thought was nothing special). It sounds crazy writing it, but that was our only issue – our own insecurities as parents. I remember reading a book called *The Mask of Motherhood* by Susan Maushart.[1] She wondered why mothers didn't help each other more, and instead, put on their best faces for the world, pretending they had it all together. As a result of this behaviour, mothers critically judge themselves in private despair – each thinking, 'I must be the only one who doesn't have it all together!'

Though Karen and I became sisters as we lived together, we struggled talking about each other's parenting. It's the most important thing in the world, but the thing we feel least qualified for. I think this is why there are so many parenting books: it's easier to read than talk about it. When our boys were young, I devoured parenting books and formed strong opinions. When my husband, who didn't read any books, disagreed with the books – we had trouble! We eventually worked out that the root of this was my insecurity as a parent.

I didn't trust that my parents had modelled parenting well, so I had to learn how to do it from a book. Brian enjoyed his childhood and felt content that it would all work out, so he didn't need advice.

A couple of decades on and I have mellowed in my strong opinions. Parenting is not an exact science and is mostly about love and vegetables. So, perhaps, it's ironic that I'm now writing a book for parents, but I hope it's simply recognising that this is how it is for us in our fast and nuclear-family world. We may like the idea of a village to raise our children, but failing that, we can draw ideas and encouragement from a book with a village in it.

For most of human history (and in many places in the world today) people lived in villages of about 150 people, which is the most social relationships our brain can maintain well. Children grew up knowing most of the people in their village. If someone's house burnt down, the children would know and could physically do something to help. Maybe they would take over some food. Maybe they would help rebuild a house. They had both relationships and agency. This cooperation between people is what has helped us thrive as a species. You've heard the saying 'It takes a village to raise a child'. In a village, a child had people who knew them and cared about them everywhere they went (I imagine at the sacrifice of privacy). Aunties, grandfathers, cousins and mentors helped raise kids.

In our urban Western world, though, we're much more likely to live in a city. A psychology experiment showed the difference between a city and a village.[2] In a busy city street, an actor pretended to fall down from a heart attack. People literally stepped around him! When he did the same thing in a village, though, everything stopped. Everyone came out onto the street to help.

In a city we're all walking around stressed because we're around so many people who don't care about us. British anthropologist Robin Dunbar's research showed that our brain gets frightened when we're around more than 150 people. [3] How many people do you have in your address book? People that you know care about you and would come to help? Probably not more than 150, right? In addition to being around more people than our brains can handle, we live in nuclear family environments instead of extended family environments. Around the world and in Indigenous communities, aunties and elders still help raise children, but it's become less common, and consumerism and technology now play a big role in influencing our children. All of these changes from village to city life can cause problems raising children.

Yet, as parents, we'd like to leave this world better than we found it. We want our kids to have an even better life than we did, and we want the world to be safe for them. But it's pretty hard to solve systemic problems like poverty, long-term war and other kinds of violence. Since people aren't born violent – it's learned behaviour – we need to stop teaching violence. And our kids will only be safe when everyone else's are too. So we'll have to start with preventing rather than curing. In order to prevent the behaviour, we need a world with a lot of people who also care, because we can't do it all alone by sheer willpower. At any time, the dominant child-rearing practices of a culture determine the quality of that society in a genera-tion's time. So, it seems to me, the most effective way for me to make this world better is to focus on raising caring chil-dren – caring about themselves, about others, and about the world around them.

To look into some aspects of the future, we do not need projec-tions by supercomputers. Much of the next millennium can be seen in how we care for our children today. Tomorrow's world may be influenced by science and technology, but more than anything, it is already taking shape in the bodies and minds of our children.

- Kofi Annan (Former Secretary-General of the United Nations)

INTRODUCTION

How to Change the World, One Family at a Time

The overall purpose of human communication is - or should be - reconciliation. It should ultimately serve to lower or remove the walls of misunderstanding which unduly separate us human beings, one from another.

> - M. Scott Peck, The Different Drum:
> Community Making and Peace

It's easy to get overwhelmed by all the problems in the world, let alone the problems in our lounge rooms. We're spending so much time on our devices or at the mall because it seems to help block it all out, but it's often a temporary and unsatisfying fix. What if you and your family could find a way to face some of the world's challenges head-on? If you could talk together about how you'd like to make this world a better place? Imagine family conversations that dealt gently with conflict. Imagine talking intelligently about cultural influences. Imagine your family participating with purpose in the world. I'm imagining your family learning together the importance of listening, practising forgiveness and creativity together, and caring about justice and what really makes us happy.

How this book came about

In some ways, this book is my story. The family I grew up in was broken, and I saw that the world was broken in many ways too. I wanted to fix it. When I had my own children, I researched frantically, unwilling to take my parenting skills for granted. My career led me into the twin concerns of educating children and eradicating poverty. I've taught children from kindergarten to university. I've encouraged Australians to understand both the effects of poverty and the highly effective solutions we've found to overcome it. I've been in awe of children's ability to understand justice and to act with great compassion. I've seen groups of people work tirelessly advocating for the rights of others who have much less power than they do. And I've seen multinational corporations change their ways as a result!

My eclectic career started in computer science. Whilst it financed my travels and introduced me to my future husband, I realised it didn't satiate my desire to make this world a better place. I retrained in psychology and then theology and began teaching. I've taught in high school, primary school, psychology for the workplace, in churches, and at universities.

I researched parenting like a true academic by reading a pile of books. Being part of a community with girlfriends leading the way helped the most. I dedicated myself to the task of child-raising, finding it difficult and lonely and wonderful and all-consuming most days.

I worked as a consultant in children and family matters to churches across our state. There I produced resources for thinking strategically about working with and inspiring kids. I came up with ideas and resources for supporting whole families. Then, during a Master's Degree in Peace and Conflict Studies, I began to look even more broadly. I read about the influence of a whole society's dominant child-rearing practices. I studied peace education and looked at the interactions between poverty and conflict. For a while there, I could hardly bear living in a world that could make child soldiers. And, yet, wherever there is horror, there are also incredible people making things better. The way people worked to ease child soldiers back into their villages gave me hope.

My master's led into another state education and coordination role with Tearfund Australia, an aid and development organisation that supports community development projects overseas. There I met parents like me who had begun supporting Tearfund when they were young and idealistic. They were now concerned about their children being influenced by our growing culture of consumerism. They were worried for the future of generosity if we are all-consumed with consuming. To address these issues, I developed conference workshops called 'Raising Kids Who Care' and the interest of parents and teachers surprised me. We talked about having 'enough!' and helping our kids become content, rather than wanting more stuff.

With the success of the workshops, I decided to write a book. My first go at this book came as I talked to children in religious education classes about issues of social justice. We played out many of the activities in this book in classrooms, where I was amazed by the depth of insight and passion these kids had. They loved thinking about the big questions of life! (Some of the work of these children appears throughout these pages, but I have always used pseudonyms to protect their identity.) I put my lessons together in a book but couldn't imagine kids picking it up by themselves.

So I researched whether there was a need for a book for families. I tested my ideas by sending a short survey to friends on social media, asking them about their dreams and fears for their children. (You'll get the chance to read their responses and make your own in a few chapters!) I received about 250 long, but anonymous, responses to my ten questions.

Next, I surveyed a bunch of young adults I knew and admired for their willingness to contribute positively to the world around them. They shared my survey with their friends too. Soon I had an even more fascinating array of advice from people fresh from the parenting factory, able to articulate what had been helpful to them. I realised how rare this opportunity is – you're going to love it! Again, the responses were anonymous, so no names are ascribed to any of them, but they knew they could end up in my book.

As I write this book, I'm also working on a series of themed family events called The Justice Games[4]. The idea is that families share a fun experience together, then have a facilitated time to talk meaningfully about it. The pre-teen years are our best opportunity for this: they're incredibly formative and kids are still open to family conversations. I'm creating shared experiences that spark conversations about the difficult issues of life. Themed events range from conflict resolution to consumerism. From creating happiness to curing depression, from purging poverty to taming technology. Whatever our society's dominant child-rearing practices are right now will impact the whole of our society in a generation's time, so it's worth working on.

On the home front, I've raised two sons who are kind and gentle and who care deeply about the environment. They understand the influences of consumerism and they shop mostly second-hand. They understand the influence of technology and use it to work, more than to play. As a child of a broken home, I was hesitant to have my own children, but my own children are keen to be fathers, which I take as a win (and I'm keen for grandchildren!).

One son got married in a huge village-style wedding and works as a renewable energy engineer. It was a simulation game about the effect of climate change on the Pacific Islands that made him change the course of his degree and gave him this life purpose. As I write, my youngest son is somewhere out of range in a four-million-year-old rainforest that has experienced a massive bushfire this year. He's researching the effect on birdlife for his final year at university. My boys are already doing their best to make the world a better place. Knowing them would be my best advertisement for credibility to write this book (although mostly they take after their gorgeous father).

My younger son solemnly told me he wants to be able to tell his grandchildren he did everything he could to prevent climate change. This book is my way of seeking to encourage a more caring, peaceful, contented society by raising kids who believe they can achieve it. I don't have all the answers, and anyway, everyone is different. But I do know that encouraging meaningful conversations in caring families will help us all enormously.

A colleague told me that women are at their most productive from 55–60. They have fewer responsibilities, and they know who they are and what they're really good at. They simply won't settle for doing anything else. I'm trying to make that me.

I guess my reason for writing this book is to collect together all the bits of information I've gathered over the last 25 years of raising my children into young men who are indeed very caring. (And because I want a more caring world for my grandchildren!)

The purpose of this book

Don't let me add to parental guilt here – we can never be more than good enough, and love covers a multitude of ineptitude. But … if we're not intentional about raising our kids, you can be sure the advertising industry will be. Marketing to children is big business and 'pester power' is harnessed to work on parents. This includes social media – of course, these pervasive technologies are also in the business of advertising. Although fabulous technological advances help our lives, we're still struggling to manage all the repercussions. Our children's lives have changed so much from our own childhoods that it's hard to keep up with what's influencing them, let alone what we should do about it. Lives are lonelier, communities more superficial and even our wealth is affecting us in ways we didn't anticipate. We are all social creatures who need to connect with others. Yet, even families struggle to maintain deep connections in our hectic lifestyles.

But knowledge is power. These cultural influences can only control us if we fail to notice them. Once we see them, we can decide for ourselves what influences we choose to include in our family life. Once we're aware of the negatives, we can take steps to prioritise the positive influences in our family culture. And once we strengthen our family communication, we can weather any storms. Then WE become the primary influence over the precious lives of our children.

This book will help you reclaim your family. **This book will provide you with a process to facilitate deep family conversations about critical social issues.** I'll give you a structure and resources to step you all through a range of themes that matter. This, in itself, will strengthen the fabric of society! A bold claim? Once we've empowered our kids to understand the world, they're in a better position to challenge it. Then they'll be able to make their own decisions about their values and directions. Our conversations can help them believe in their own ability to act on their desires, to care about others and to contribute to the world around them.

I've been part of a local church community for three decades. Together we've struggled with the influences of our culture. As parents, we have tried to build a culture of contentment and compassion and contribution. I've been around long enough to see the fruit of our labours. Children I've known since they were born are now working in community development work. They work with Indigenous communities and in homeless shelters. Some are in international aid and development organisations. They're marching for climate action and visiting politicians. These young adults inspire me and give me great hope for the future of their world.

These fabulous young people explain the effect their parents had on their lives:

- *My parents were able to make us feel like we could talk about anything with them. I always thought that was quite extraordinary, and it helped me immensely.*

- *My mum was always super open and honest. We had a close relationship, and she always treated me like an adult, which helped me in being able to talk to her about my issues openly and honestly. This always meant that I was never sheltered away from these real-life issues and could attempt to deal with them like a mature adult.*

- *They put effort into trying to show us how we fit into the wider world. This included a trip to Vietnam and lots of lessons about the poor.*

- *They have always been good at trying to see it from my point of view and respecting that I can make the right decision for myself.*

- *My father once disclosed to me some of his personal struggles with depression as I was going through it myself. I had never known, and it was probably the first real conversation we've had together.*

- *They continually teach me to value preserving this Earth we are on. Whether it be by excessively recycling, valuing other people's discarded material possessions or in the way they tell me 'Put more clothes on!' when I complain about being cold in our non-heated house. I just love the way I've been brought up to have an ethical/environmental conscience.*

- *They encouraged me in adventure and pursuits I never thought I'd be capable of doing and then got the chance to do.*

Parents matter! It's hard to tell which will be our most teachable moments, amongst the rough and tumble of daily family life, but they are always in there … for better or worse.

By using the conversations in this book with your family, you will

- deepen the level of your teachable moments.
- discover thoughts you didn't know your children had, and they will amaze you!
- develop a connection and a direction that the whole family will find deeply satisfying.
- make decisions together as a family about what is important, what needs limits and what those limits should be.

And your kids will

- own these decisions because they've been part of the process.
- develop agency – an understanding of the world around them and how they can contribute to it.

If you are someone who cares about other people and wants your kids to care too, then this book is for you. If you've had enough of the consumerist story that says going to the mall will make you happy, stay with me. If you want your kids to learn to find contentment in life, then read on. But if you want your kids to become billionaires, there are plenty of other good books out there!

Our time with our kids is limited. I know, I know, I didn't believe this either. Preschool years seemed to last forever. Now that empty nest is upon me, though, and I have raised young men who can cope well in the world without me, I realise how precious that time with them was. The time when they are willing to learn from us and with us is short too! While primary schools like parents to be involved, hanging around high school is out of the question! So don't wait until your kids are old enough for big conversations. Instead, start building a culture of communication when they're young, and it will keep you all talking right through the turbulent teen years. Build a foundation when they are young, and your investment will pay off not only in their lives but in their contribution as great citizens.

This is not just another parenting book – it's a book for families. I have curated research for parents and conversations or activities for families to put that research into practise. And I'm suggesting that your kids lead the family times – so I'm addressing those sections to them! I've broken the book into four big areas of life:

- Our Relationships (mostly in our family)
- Our Culture (mostly our mind and attitudes)
- Our Inner Selves (mostly our character and souls)
- Our World (mostly how we can find purpose and help the world!)

Of course, I'm using family here in a very wide sense. **Every family looks different.** Some families are bigger than others. Some are small and some are blended. Kids of different ages and stages. Various mixtures of parents and relatives. Maybe you're an aunt or a grandparent or a carer reading this? No problem – same conversations. Whatever the shape of your family or classroom or youth group these ideas can help.

This is a practical book – it will improve your family communication and purpose – but it will only work if you have the talks. I can give you the reasons why and the tools to do it, but it will only work if you enthuse your family to get into it. This might be hard at first, but I promise it will get easier as everyone realises it's fun and worthwhile. When I taught kids, they loved talking about the meaning of life. Remember asking 'When will I ever use this algebra formula in real life?!' They won't say that about the conversations in this book. They'll say, 'At last – this is real life!'

If you're someone who likes theory and reading research, then read the parents' section. If you are busy and want to start experimenting right away, you can jump straight to the family sections. I'm assuming you already want kids who care? This book is about how to help it happen!

How to use this book

In part one, **Where We're Headed**, we'll look at two surveys – one taken by parents and one by young adults who've recently experienced the effects of parenting! This will also be an opportunity for you to consider what your struggles and dreams are in your parenting. Then I'll give an overview of each of the relational areas.

In part two, **On the Road**, each of our relationship areas (with each other, with our culture, with ourselves and with the world) has two chapters: a chapter for you (parent, grandparent, or carer) that contains questions to inspire your thinking, and a chapter for the kids to lead the family activities and conversations.

Feel free to pick and choose according to what fits your family, and to change the language as you go. The conversations are really just there to spark your own conversations – and give you an excuse to have them!

1. Read through the parents' sections of the book. Then think about what your family needs most right now. You can either work right through the conversations in the family section as they appear, or you can jump to any that appeal to you.

2. Pick a time in the week that works and make it a new family tradition to have structured conversation time. You could do it over dinner or for an hour afterwards. You

could pick a rainy weekend afternoon or long car drive. You could race through them quickly or meander. Consider making a regular family date time to dive into this meaningful fun!

3. Get each person in the family a scrapbook or sketch pad of their own and some colourful pens or felt pens to write or draw initial thoughts or responses to the conversations. Really! I'll refer to this often! (It will help young ones and introverts gather their thoughts so they'll have more to say).

4. Encourage your kids to lead the family conversations in the book. They can take turns reading and sharing out the instructions. Treat this as a responsibility and a privilege. Tell your kids that you will need their creativity and energy (as yours is in short supply!) The activities are written assuming children who can read will be leading. This means they should be very easy to follow. Check everyone understands anyway. You may like to read through beforehand to provide your own personal examples along the way. Feel free to bring in your own knowledge and stories – the idea is just to get you all talking!

5. Remember the aim is to grow your family culture of open communication and purpose as you work together on your family mission to improve the world! There are no rules here – each family is unique and makes their own decisions about what's important to them. The activities can just be conversation starters – go with the flow if you get into a useful side-topic. Follow your family's interests.

6. Set some ground rules together – your kids will have done this in their classrooms at school so can probably lead this process too! Start with things like no talking over the top of someone else. Find ways to ensure everyone gets an equal opportunity to speak (loud people need quiet times; quiet people need their moment). You'll probably need to add to this list as you go!

7. Follow up throughout the week. Ask how everyone did. Were there skills to practise or actions to take? Perhaps there was some research to do? Think about ways to keep it fun – even surprising. Perhaps ice-cream will help? Perhaps you might use some ideas for holiday activities? Perhaps invite a guest or another family sometimes? Watch for things that happen in your lives that could connect to the activities to help embed them in the reality of life.

8. Get your kids to read the following instructions about the structure that will shape every conversation in this book. In fact, this whole book is shaped around this idea of a journey. Before we set off on our family adventure, we think about where we're headed, what we'll need to pack, instructions for how to get there, conversations for the trip, then we share memories as we unpack. Whether your family is taking a short trip or planning for the journey of life together, I trust these conversations will help you get there with hope and joy.

Visit www.raisingkidswhocare.info to download a printable version of the conversation template for everyone to write their notes.

Notes for Children Before Starting the Conversations

You are probably much more familiar with being creative than your parents, so they might need your guidance.

1. You can do this by taking leadership of the conversation activities. Read out the instructions and encourage everyone to give it a try.

2. Feel free to ask any extra questions or talk about whatever is on your mind at the moment instead of sticking exactly to the instructions.

3. At the end of each conversation (and sometimes it'll be suggested at the start), draw or write a response in your notebook.

4. Maybe you could make a poster to help the family remember what you've all learnt or agreed upon?!

5. All of the conversations for families will have a similar format to make things clear. They are formatted in a way to suggest you're getting ready for a holiday or an outing.

Conversation Title

 ## 1. Where we're headed

* First, you'll want to know where you're off to: the end goal of the conversation.
* What are you hoping to see or learn?

 ## 2. Packing our bags: what we need to know, or something to stimulate our thinking

* Now you can pack the things you'll need for the trip.
* Will you need swimmers or a book? Coloured pens or modelling clay?
* What do you need to know or think about first?

 ## 3. Reading the map: instructions or preparation

* Then you'll read the map – your instructions for how to get there or any preparation for the trip.

 ## 4. On the road: our conversation

* And you're off for your holiday or activity!
* Time to just do it.

5. Unpacking

* When you're back or finished, you'll need to unpack.
* You'll share memories, talking about the best bits or the worst bits.

6. Making the journey matter

* Maybe you learnt a new skill on your trip. What might help you to practise so you can keep it up? What will you do differently now in your real lives?

PART I

WHERE WE'RE HEADED

It is intoxicating to be caught up in the next new thing, to be seen as alternative or visionary, but the real encounter is often found in a conversation over the washing up.

- Celtic Daily Prayer

You really shouldn't say 'I love you' unless you mean it. But if you mean it, you should say it a lot. People forget.

- Jill, (8)

CHAPTER 1

PACKING OUR BAGS

What will our kids need to make the journey of life?

Sean Sumner is a physical therapist who wanted to write a book. His eight-year-old daughter, Emma, was very interested in what he was doing and said she wanted to write a book too. He sent her off, telling her to come back when she'd written 150 words and had some characters. Then he got back to work. Emma soon arrived back with 175 words, 10 characters and a story outline! At that point, he started taking her more seriously. They built a Saturday morning tradition of going to a local coffee shop to write their books together. They got some more people involved over Facebook, updating them on their progress. They encouraged each other when it got hard and planned rewards like contacting cover designers when they met their goals. Sean realised this was project-based learning. And it was fun! They both published, and as you can imagine, Emma got lots of local publicity. She's even been asked to make author visits to schools. They donate to charity from her earnings. Emma grew in confidence and kept writing.[5] Kids respond extremely well to challenges, especially if we get involved, dedicating our time to help them.

In our busy culture, we can miss experiencing the joy of learning together as a family and of project-based learning. **As parents, we often underestimate the developmental level of our 'babies'.** Sean could have underestimated Emma, but he gave her a chance. Our kids are usually a step ahead of us because we can't comprehend how on earth they have grown up so fast. They're also learning so many new things at school that we haven't taught them. We used to be in charge of everything!

By working with your kids on these family activities, you will have a window into their progress again. You'll be amazed at their wisdom. You'll also have the opportunity to share your own life knowledge that might not otherwise come up in the helter-skelter of busy life. Working together will let you skill up together as a family, making you more connected, with better communication. Most exciting, you will be able to set plans together for contributing to the world around you.

Before you undertake this exciting adventure, think about what you want your kids to become when they grow up. I remember sitting in a friend's glamorous kitchen in a wealthy suburb as she bemoaned the materialistic tendencies of her kids. She and her husband came from hard-working immigrant families. They'd given their children more than they'd ever had, but now she was realising this meant they hadn't learnt to appreciate it.

By contrast, I heard an Australian mother speak about what it was like to bring up her kids in Cairo. She was a midwife with four children, long, long hair, and visible serenity. She said she really liked being away from home because it gave her a lot more control over what distractions influenced her children. In Cairo, she was more able to monitor access to television and computer games. What she liked most, though, was that her children were much more likely to become involved in overseas development work by growing up in a less-developed country. These 'third-culture' kids are tolerant and inclusive – they learn empathy by being outsiders themselves. 'Well, isn't that what we all want for our children?' the beautiful midwife asked her wealthy, white audience. Or do we want them to become doctors and lawyers and make lots of money?!

Of course, we may not share her values, but it's a good question, isn't it? Here's an even more provocative idea: 'Imagine who you want your kids to become. Be that.' We know that it's our modelling that's likely to have the most profound influence on our children – whether we realise it or not.

So what do you want for your kids?

- To have a good career?
- To be happy?
- To search for happiness in the right places?
- To be financially free?
- To talk confidently?
- To be successful?
- To be married?
- To resolve conflict?
- To think clearly and creatively?
- To be resilient?
- To care deeply about others and to know how to help them?

What else ... ? Perhaps good grades, good friends, athletic ability, kindness, humour, creativity, and curiosity about the world, or art, music, literature?

Can you think of a time your child amazed you?

How have you amazed them?

A parenting survey

A while ago I thought I'd see whether I was the only one thinking about how to raise kids who care. I put up a simple survey on Facebook and was amazed at the response. I got hundreds of long answers from parents and from young adults. Before I share their thoughts, why don't you take the survey yourself?

Questions will refer to 'your child' as opposed to 'your children' for clarity, but feel free to respond with any or all of your children in mind.

1. In what ways does your child amaze you or give you joy?

_____

_____

_____

2. **Which of these issues are you concerned about for your child?**

Issue	Not worried	Unsure	A bit worried	Very worried
Lack of community support				
Peer group pressure				
Anxiety/depression				
Consumerism				
Technology				
Pornography				
Communication				
Self-centredness				
Self-agency/belief in their ability to act on the world				
Other:				

3. **Does your family have specific ways to deal with any of these issues?**

_____

_____

_____

4. **Please rank your desires for your child:**
   - Academic success
   - Good citizenship
   - Relationship success
   - Financial success
   - Achieving their own goals
   - Other:

5. **What's one opportunity or event that has helped your child grow as a person?**

_____

_____

_____

6. Is your child interested in …

	Never	Sometimes	Often
Politics			
Fundraising for charity			
Caring for friends			
The environment			
Gadgets/games/fashion			
Social justice			
Other			

7. What might your mission statement as a parent be?

_____

_____

_____

I think parents responded abundantly because, let's face it, we are obsessed with our kids. It gets old for other people, so it's a treat when we find a new audience! But not all the obsessive thoughts are positive. Parents spend a lot of time worrying about their children. One study found that parents spend more than five hours a day worrying – often in the middle of the night![6] The study reported the top three worries: children's safety, happiness and then bullying. With the existence of real influences beyond our control, it makes sense that we worry.

A government relationship-support organisation in Australia says parents worry about safety and health, social media and bullying, school and their children's future, discipline, _and how to talk to their children!_[7] They agreed that if children are loved and cared for, the exact parenting style used doesn't matter. Like me, they suggest that talking with our children about life will build trust and show interest before the complexity of teenage years when it's really needed.

A large 'Guiding Children' report from 2020[8] found that **the top parenting struggles were relational** (which is why one of our conversations will be about conflict resolution) and included peer pressure and busyness. Family time and communication are diminishing in our current culture. Technology struggles were also highlighted and included inappropriate digital content, video games and social media.

Another large study looked at the main values parents wanted their children to have.[9] Teaching children to be responsible was ranked highest, then hard work and helping others. Opinions varied after that, but some of the values were creativity, empathy for others and curiosity. We'll be looking at these in this book.

To combat these issues, research, from the longest study ever, suggests we spend time with children, let them make decisions and maintain a happy family.[10] Doing chores is cited as teaching children they need to contribute to the good of the whole. Further research also found a significant correlation between the social skills of very young children and their success as adults twenty years later.

My survey was not a scientific study and was a bit leading, but I found it **fascinating hearing from other parents.** I realised how rare this is. As I said earlier, we're all worried we are the only ones struggling. Knowing that these struggles are normal is a huge help in managing our fears. It also helps to hear the variety of ways other parents have dealt with their concerns, as it sparks our own ideas. Of course, I can't reproduce all of it here, and I'm told not everyone finds it as interesting as I do, so I've given you some more examples in an appendix. I encourage you to at least have a look!

Until then, here's a summary of the responses I received.

Q1: It was heart-warming to hear parents' joy was most often about the goodness of children.

My eldest son brings me great joy when he is kind to others. He will always stop to help another child that has hurt themselves or needs assistance. Kindness is a beautiful thing to watch.

Q2: The issues parents are worried about didn't differ very much in amount – they pretty much worried a bit about all of the things I'd proposed! There were two broad clusters though. They were most worried about peer group pressure, early sexualisation/porn, and anxiety/depression then consumerism and technology. Less worrying were communication skills and community support.

Absolutely worried (about peer group pressure). This is one of the biggest things that any young person has to navigate in growing up.

Working in a school, I see first-hand the influence that pornography has on both boys and girls. This is going to be one of the biggest issues that social workers and the health system will be dealing with in the next decade I feel ...

Q3: The number one response to the ways families deal with these issues was 'Talking with kids'. Whether through family meetings or while in the car or through a culture of open communication, this was the primary tool parents used to tackle difficult issues.

I am always asking my children for ways in which I can improve at being their parent. This gives them the confidence that our relationship is two way, and they feel secure telling me anything, knowing I will guide not school. We deal with the issues together.

Complete openness and honesty, treating the children with respect, honouring their individuality and their right to be themselves, equal rights to everyone within the family ... all of these were important.

Taking age-appropriate responsibilities and allowing consequences also featured, as did having clear family values. More practically, limiting screen time, doing fun things together, role modelling, volunteering or second-hand shopping, and seeking professional help when needed.

Q4: There was very little differentiation in what we desire for our children. The most common were empathy and compassion, then contentment, gratitude and being comfortable with themselves. Contentment was more important than happiness.

The most noteworthy difference was what was least desired: financial success and then academic success. This is a good indication that we are all on the same page about our intentions for our children, but we need to be vigilant about the effect our culture has on what success looks like.

Q5: In the question asking what has most helped their child grow as a person, encouraging volunteering opportunities were the standout comments!

> *Getting involved in volunteer activities e.g. Clean up Australia, packing Christmas hampers, food drives and helping out friends when they need it. Has given them the sense that they can make a difference in the world.*

Nurturing younger siblings or pets, coaching and being part of a community were also credited.

Q6: Our children were interested in 'caring for friends' then 'gadgets and games' miles ahead of the other responses. Environment, charity, fashion and social justice were 'sometimes'. Politics, you guessed it, was the highest 'never'.

Q7: My favourite was hearing parents articulate what they really cared about. The survey's Mission Statements were amazing and will feature in the 'Caring for Our World' chapter, where you'll have an opportunity to work on your own family mission statement!

- *To bring up my children to be the best possible people they can be – healthy, happy and contributing to society.*

- *To raise children who are being participants in the world rather than observers.*

- *To build resilience, develop respect and encourage faith through modelling this ourselves.*

- *Life preparation. Shenanigans. Teaching them to think and be self-reliant. I suck at mission statements.*

Advice from caring, justice-minded young adults

Do you remember being an idealistic young person looking for meaning and purpose in life? Concerned about social injustices and wondering why your parents were so conservative? Then parenthood came and you realised why social norms are normal. Stability is good for children and their exhausted parents! A decade or two later though, those exhausted parents may have forgotten their ideals somewhat. This shows we each need to stay open to the truths and insights of different generations. So much of life is about balance, isn't it?

A large research project called The Connected Generation interviewed 15,000 young adults in 25 countries in late 2019.[11] They found the digitally connected young adults were also lonely. They had a surprising openness towards spirituality, possibly connected to their perception of human suffering and global conflict. These young people had grown up in a fast-changing and sometimes chaotic world. Now, they are longing to make a significant difference. They want to be part of something useful, with the opportunity to fight injustice alongside friends. They also want to see evidence of adults 'practising what they preach'.

I received responses from 38 young adults to a survey of my own, with similar types of questions as the parents' one. I know these young people personally – some for their whole lives – and I can attest to their caring-ness! This survey gave me fabulous insight into the often unknown effects of our parenting. Remember that I specifically picked **young people who were already caring and justice minded.**

What they cared about

Caring for friends was their highest concern, but next was social justice and the environment. **Volunteering was very high too – not one person left this off their list!**

Gadgets, games and fashion were very low for these kids and social media was only 'sometimes' cared about.

Who most influenced them to care

Parents was the clear winner here! This should fill us with both confidence and trepidation at our big responsibility. Friends and church were the next biggest influences. Most talked about this happening through simple role modelling.

How their parents shaped their character

They gave wonderful concrete examples of the ways parents shaped their character to be more caring.

Empathy:

> *Whenever we complained about something/someone, they would almost always get us to try to think about it from the other person's perspective.*

> *Encouraging us to accept invitations to parties or spend time with people who other people didn't like to spend time with – it helped me to value looking out for people on the edge.*

Experience:

> *Habits cultivate character, right? So, in teaching me habits such as asking others if they want a drink, genuinely asking people how they are, and encouraging good stewardship, my parents shaped my character to be more caring.*

Modelling:

> *They used to have a lot of people who were a little on the outer for lunch or dinner and host them like a celebrity. We were all encouraged to sit at the table and take part in the conversation.*

> *Purely by example. Seeing the way my parents interacted with their friends and the public. Teaching me that it is a great quality to be able to give without expecting anything in return.*

Generosity:

They have encouraged me to be humble, generous and compassionate; to be aware of myself and who I am, but to put the needs and welfare of others above my own. One way they did this was to give me a structured way to 'deal with' my pocket money; some went into a bank account, some I could put in a piggy bank for something I was saving for, and some I had to put in a separate container for church (I got to choose which ministry at church that money would go to at the end of the month).

Their reflections on the issues that concern parents:

Peer group pressure:

I did a lot of things that I don't agree with now because of pressure from peers.

My parents let us use them as scapegoats if we ever didn't want to do something.

Consumerism:

They wouldn't feed into my consumerist nature and limited the stuff they bought me which meant I had to work for it. Mum would also always chat to me about the big issues giving me gentle reminders.

Technology:

Can be distracting and also a social pressure to keep up with trends.

Dad programmed the computer to say [in a robot voice], 'Get off now. You have been on the computer for 3 hrs, 37 mins and 42 seconds.'

Early sexualisation and porn:

High school makes you 'grow up' real quick in that regard because of everything that everyone else has seen/knows about and shares.

My parents were able to make us feel like we could talk about anything with them. I always thought that was quite extraordinary, and it helped me immensely in this area.

Communication:

I found it difficult to open up to people about things that were really personal to me, because I feared shame, vulnerability and rejection.

Self-confidence:

I've always had very poor self-confidence, but my parents (mum especially) have always believed in me and helped to give me confidence.

Notice here the importance of talking with your children. I was talking to a friend in her mid-twenties recently. She has a fabulous family – close, committed, community-minded. My friend said her parents modelled a good life well. But she can't remember them ever having explicit conversations about things that matter. She is struggling with some issues now, and she wonders why her parents didn't talk to her about them?

Their advice to help parents who want to raise kids who care

Get ready to take notes from this rare opportunity to hear wisdom from the type of young people we're hoping our kids will grow into!

Model

Model those values – don't shelter your kids from the world but take them with you into it, so that you can demonstrate to them compassion, welcome and courage :)

Listen

Be sensitive to them, listen to what they have to say, and try not to make arguments out of things that didn't need to be arguments. If parents exhibit these qualities, children will surely be able to see the positive difference it makes in their relationship with their parents, and then (hopefully) be encouraged to act similarly in their relationships with friends and people they meet along the way.

Expose

If you can take your children travelling, do it! If not, get them to volunteer. Also working helps as you learn the value of money.

Do things that one who cares about the world would do, and then do them with your kids.

Limit

Less technology, more imagination – books, art and music, give them time to be bored.

To encourage your children to be 'in' the world; don't let them spend time on screens, but encourage them to facilitate real friendships, and to explore real emotions and have real adventures.

Love

I feel that most parents see their children as meaning the world to them. Don't be afraid to show that. Showing love is one of the most important things a parent can do. Play with your kids and encourage them to play with other children.

Be present in your children's lives. And love anyone and everyone.

I hope you've enjoyed reading the thoughts of other parents and the advice of young people as much as I did. These are the aims we'll work towards throughout this book. It's my hope and prayer that your family will enjoy the journey, and that the world will benefit from it! Let's go!

CHAPTER 2

READING THE MAP

Finding the best way through life.

Four relational areas to visit together

I've divided the whole of life into four sections! Who knew it was so easy?! Of course, this is pretty arbitrary and we're complex creatures, but bear with me. While we are holistic, not-completely-rational people and all of our parts are a mess of interconnections, I think it will help if we consider the lives of our kids through the lenses of their relationships, their cultural influences, their inner selves and their purpose in the world. There will, of course, be overlap, but this might help you choose where your family could focus first.

Our relationships

To grow young people who care and will be cared for, the first thing we have to do is help them get their relationships working well. We all need to feel secure, to feel loved, to feel safe and to know how to be loving people with good friendships. No matter what our kids end up doing in life, the quality of their relationships will decide how much fun they have, and how much extra energy they have to contribute to the world (the less energy spent on trying to get their needs met, the more they have). Love's ultimately what will give them a happy life, right?

This will involve knowing how to listen well to others and how to manage conflict well. Forgiveness and hospitality will feature. In short, we'll need to get their **hearts** loved up. We'll consider how to build resilience by strengthening their relationship skills. We'll prepare them to build community by learning how to build good heart-fulfilling relationships.

Our culture

Often the only thing we have control of in our life is our attitude. We can choose whether to accept or challenge our mood. We can choose whether to give up or to persevere. We can choose to think the best of people or to judge and criticise. Our perspective can make a big difference in how we face situations in life. Think 'first-world problem'.

We also need to be clear about how our society might be getting in the way. We're swimming around in our culture, not always aware of the effect that it's having on us. In Western culture that effect is pretty strong, and not always ideal for raising kids who care, so we'll need to help them have clear **minds**. Building an awareness of our cultural influences is a key step, so we'll look at things like consumerism and technology.

Our inner selves

How do we know the best way to have a happy and meaningful life? What goals should we be pursuing? We will take a look at this pursuit of happiness. Sometimes life will get hard along the way, despite our resistance to this idea in Western culture. Naively, we seem to think we can all be rich and famous and ignore pain and death. But bad stuff happens to everyone. We will look at why some people cope better than others when it does.

Much work has been done in positive psychology recently to understand character traits. They confirm what many religions also encourage to help a person cope: traits like wisdom, generosity and courage. We'll think about how **character and spiritedness** are best formed so our kids will have strength for life's journey.

Our world

Next, they'll need to know what direction to head in to have **purposeful** lives. Meaning and purpose contribute to our happiness in life. We'll look at examples of missions or causes we could follow to help us grow a sense of agency and purpose, caring for the **world** on the way!

Being clear about what is and what isn't a problem is important too, so we'll look at some of the ways we can think factually. Unfortunately, many of us have lost hope that an individual can make a difference in the world today. It's not true. We can do several exciting things that actually do make a very real difference. Doing so will build a worldview in our kids that says 'I can do something about that problem', and then the world will really start to change!

Combining all of these traits will help our children become kids who care and who are contributing to making the planet a better place. And once your kids want to care about the world, it's pretty inspiring and gets us as parents on board as well!

Format

The way we'll do it is first I'll have a chat with you, the parents and carers, to help you to get thinking about what your best intentions are and how to achieve them. Then you'll have conversational activities for your families to do together to start turning those intentions into actions.

One of the most effective ways to make this happen is to **get the kids to lead these family times.** I've written the family activities with this in mind. Having the kids lead will benefit them in many ways: they are much more likely to want to get involved, they will enjoy bossing their parents about and they'll get leadership experience.

Psychologists talk about our 'Locus of Control' to measure the extent of control we think we have over outcomes in our lives.[12] This is a spectrum: at one end we feel like victims, with our fate out of our control; at the other end of the spectrum, we're narcissists who think we are the master of the universe! Clearly, somewhere in the middle is ideal. Children often have less (perceived and real) control than adults in the world. Giving them opportunities to act on their environment will help them grow more influence over their lives. It's also not helpful for children to think they are the centre of the universe if we want to help them learn to care for others. The activities in this book will give them control for the purpose of caring for others. They'll strike a good balance in our kids between agency and empathy. And they'll make the world better along the way!

Theories of change

To inspire your thinking in each relational area, I will ask and answer three questions in each of the four main sections:

- **How are we going now?** (This is what the culture we're swimming in is like, and the effect it's having on our families)
- **What can we imagine would be better?** (Dream and imagine what a better future might be like)
- **What can we change to get there?** (The tools or skills we can use to help our families along their journey. This is our 'theory of change'. It's our hypothesis about what will help. The big idea here is that we can bring about change if we're intentional and if we're communicative about this with our family.)

For example, imagine a family full of conflict. People yelling, doors slamming. No one wants to share, and the most dominant person gets their way the most. Someone comes in crying because a toy is missing and they blame a sibling. This would be an unpleasant reality!

Imagine a better way … the house is quiet, siblings are sharing and caring for each other, the family listens to the crying child and that child listens as someone explains calmly what happened to the toy. They come up with a mutually agreeable solution. The family learns from new perspectives and respects the diversity behind them.

How do we get there? It even sounds unrealistic as I type! Clearly, it may not happen overnight, but skills exist to help us deal with conflict well. It's a normal part of life, after all, so we might as well get good at it! The family spends some time together learning to listen well, a skill that they can work on anytime. Then they learn basic mediation skills. They learn to seek first to understand, and then to be understood. Magic happens when they spend time understanding a problem from another point of view. They learn that communication is the best tool we have for resolving conflict.

Let's think about these three questions from a wider perspective now.

1. How are we going now?

We'll look at the reality of life for our children and families in our current culture, using research findings and real-life stories. For example, corporate greed is rampant in both Western societies and the developing world. This greed looks like consumerism targeting children. It looks like all-pervasive technology and social media. It has dire consequences for poorly paid workers in the developing world. Interestingly enough, our own wealth is influencing us in unhelpful ways. Research shows children are experiencing anxiety and depression at alarming rates. Big corporate organisations and government decisions leave us feeling powerless and frustrated. In our world, a few have obscene wealth, while others don't have enough share in the resources of our planet to sustain life, let alone to flourish.

All that said, people are amazingly resilient. Change is coming as the younger generation starts to reject traditional power and a movement begins for change.

2. What can we imagine would be better?

We all need inspiration for our life journey. The world is full of good news stories, but whenever we see a disaster, the news reports focus on what's sensationally bad. In every case though, we could just as easily look for the heroes who are there helping. People are capable of great things because we are capable of imagining a better world. In each section, we'll imagine what could be better than our current reality.

For example, imagine if kids were educated to care about themselves, about others and about the world?! Imagine if families knew how to build a culture of communication and conflict resolution and purpose. Imagine if kids had the skills to understand consumerism and push back against it. Robin Grille, psychologist and author of *Parenting for a Peaceful World* puts it like this:

> *Human behaviour is more free and changeable by far than that of any other animal, and to a large extent, violence is a learned response passed down from generation to genera-tion... The way is open for us to create the kind of societies we want, once we understand how relationship styles emerge from emotional development in children.*[13]

Imagine if whole societies had children raised to care – there would be less hate and war and suffering!

3. What can we change to get there?

Now that we're all fired up, how do we actually achieve our heart's desires? Simple goal setting says we work backwards in progressively smaller steps. This book does that, as **the basic premise is that starting with the family is not only prevention, it's the cure.** To create children who flourish and help others flourish, we need to help our kids cultivate healthy emotional intelligence, an awareness of their world and their place in it and a worldview that says they can enact change in their world! The family activities in this book are designed to be the first steps along the path to our imagined future. In each section, we'll look at what we can do to get families started on the journey to a better future together.

Change starts with every intentional family conversation.

Family conversations

This section contains the family activities related to the big four relational areas. The conversations will be addressed to your children because **I'm hoping to encourage you to let them lead the activities!** This should help the kids get involved, make it less 'teachery' and give your kids some good leadership opportunities along the way!

'Kids' is a loose term, I realise. For primary school–aged children to lead, they will need to be able to read! That said, families are fabulously diverse, and you know yours better than anyone. I can picture you helping younger children get involved at their own level.

Teenagers would actually get the most out of the activities and have much to offer you. You might find that structured conversations help them talk. The subject matter may be things they really care about at an age when they're thinking about big things in life. Knowing you care about these too (and not just clean rooms and vegetables!) could provide a helpful bond. Young people today are deeply concerned about issues of social justice.

The importance and joy of talking with kids

A truly wonderful resource for learning to listen and talk to our children well is psychologist Robin Grille's *Heart to Heart Parenting*.[14] It is inspirational and practical – full of communication skills driven by the need to connect emotionally with our children. Grille says attention is life-giving and our children will listen to us according to how well they feel heard by us. Listening can mend broken relationships and help hearts heal, which ensures their own caring behaviour. And it sets the scene for conversational role-modelling.

When we are emotionally open with our children and when our words are congruent with our feelings, we earn their trust. This approach involves a shift of our focus from 'How do I change my child's behaviour?' to 'How do I role model the respect that I want my child to learn?'[15]

Furthermore, if we don't talk to our kids about tricky subjects, they might be left thinking that they can't talk about tricky things at home. We don't want them to wander through life picking up tips at random! The conversations here are just starters. You're building a culture that says 'we talk about everything in our family'. This will be especially helpful when you hit your kids' teenage years.

There's plenty of research that suggests working with children in this way is not only possible but desirable. For example, educators recognise that parents and carers form an integral part of school communities. There's a growing understanding of the important part that parents play in the academic achievement of their child. Parental expectation predicts student achievement. The impact of the home and parents' involvement on a child's well-being and social development is very important.[16]

Student Well-being Information in Australia lists 'student voice' as one of the key ways to support young people.[17] The practices they recommend to encourage this in schools are:

- Provide opportunities for authentic student decision making over matters that affect them
- Create and maintain inclusive and interactive learning environments to encourage active student participation to foster a sense of connectedness
- Actively engage students through the use of evidence-informed, strengths-based approaches to enhance their own learning and well-being
- Explicitly teach social and emotional skills using evidence-informed practices related to personal safety, resilience, help-seeking and protective behaviours across the curriculum
- Collaborate with students to develop strategies to enhance well-being, promote safety and counter violence, bullying and abuse in all online and physical spaces

And these practices are adaptable to the family environment. Family meetings can ensure decisions are explained to children and their viewpoints considered. One of the aims of this book is to help families grow these social and emotional skills.

We'll also look at helping them grow philosophically. Teacher and philosopher Michael Parker is interested in helping children develop ethical thinking. His book *Ethics 101: Conversations to have with your kids* has discussion questions on a range of topics from bullying to climate change, and from generosity to online etiquette.[18] He asks us as parents to consider whether we'd rather our children were smart or good? Of course, it's a both/and dilemma, but he points out how much more effort is put into the academic education of our children.

He also asks us to think outside the paradigm of our individualism so we can prepare our children to be good citizens of society. We can ask, 'What would happen if everyone behaved this way?' Children primarily learn ethical behaviour by watching their parents. Allowing them to discuss ideas and come to their own conclusions is an even more effective method of developing ethics. Parker describes it like this:

> *You can tell a child 'You have to be tolerant of other people' and he or she will hear 'parent static' and probably filter you out. But if you use situations and examples to discuss tolerance and guide them to their own conclusions your child will probably come to the view that tolerance is preferable to intolerance. The difference is that your child will have articulated the view themselves... to make them think it themselves.*[19]

That reminds me of the way aspiring authors learn to 'show don't tell'. It's more effective to let readers discover for themselves through a story rather than being preached at. Parker goes on to say that even better would be to get them to *practise* tolerance. I aim to encourage both discussion and practise with the activities in this book.

Helping kids to contribute

As you engage in these conversations, especially in the 'our world' section, remember to help your kids see how they can be involved in improving the world, their family, and their character.

Esher Wojcicki has just written a book called *How to Raise Successful People*.[20] She has great qualifications: one of her daughters is a doctor and the other two are Silicon Valley CEOs. Her main point is that people need to contribute meaningfully to the world. She says:

Everywhere there's a problem to be solved, someone or some group to support and champion. It really is a way of being in the world, and when it comes to our kids, it pays to shape this perspective as early as possible... Why do you think that here in the U.S. we have an epidemic of opioid addiction, depression and suicide? We don't seem to have the right information about how to live well, how to take care of ourselves and others. We're chasing money and possessions. Not service, not purpose. If we have a purpose at all, it's to make ourselves happy. But if there's one thing I know, it's this: You're happiest – as well as most beneficial to society – when you're doing things to help others.[21]

The challenge is to think about this as we're parenting. As we take up our causes, we teach our kids through our own modelling. We show them that we can work together to fight for the well-being of our communities. Then our children will feel empowered to contribute to the challenges of our times. Encouraging our children to get active and volunteer is going to be important too.

Esher Wojcicki quotes research that tells us:

Teenagers who volunteer with younger children experience both decreased negative moods and cardiovascular risk, according to a 2013 study. Another study, from 2016, found that teenagers who performed volunteer work were significantly less likely to engage in illegal behaviours and also had fewer convictions and arrests between the ages of 24 and 34.[22]

A cure for negative teenage moods! Just as my young adults predicted. When charities consider the demographics of their donors, they rarely consider children. But children are born with a strong sense of justice and generosity that, like a muscle, needs to be engaged and developed. Children now influence the culture, spending choices, and family values. Young people are much more engaged in advocacy actions. While children are capable of great compassion and even leadership, they're often distracted in our current culture by consumerism and screens!

When children and youth are inspired to advocate and to fundraise for others with less power, we empower them. We also engage the families and communities who want to support them.

Finally, we should get our kids involved because young adults advise it. Here are some specific reasons they give.

- *I think it's really important to make your children aware of these issues from a young age and don't sugar coat it too much. You need your child to know the realities of the world. I think always approaching conversations and questions like the child is an adult is a great way to make the child feel more empowered and like they can make a change.*

- *Understanding that it is hard, be considerate of your child's ability. Have clear boundaries and share with them (information about you, the world, your views) and encourage them to share with you.*

- *Be engaged with them and their environment, discuss issues at dinner, let them feel as though they are not separated from the world and then expected to be pushed into it. Grow with them.*

Tips for success

Michael Parker's book *Ethics 101* looks like a book for parents on one side, and for kids on the other. His introduction for the children tells his young audience that they are key players in a scheme to teach their parents about ethics. As he reminds them that their parents will need help with fresh and creative ideas, he helps them sympathise with parents who are stuck in old beliefs. Their strong sense of fairness is praised. Then he suggests they make it fun by getting pizza involved![23]

I'd suggest that the activities in this book are best approached with a sense of fun too. If we start with a belief that children can and do have great ideas to contribute – they will. **Children rise to the level of our expectations of them** – it's a psychological effect.[24] Let's give them the opportunity to amaze us.

When parents respect their children's ideas and thought processes, they encourage them to participate even more. The best way to do this is by asking good questions. We want to fan conversations into flame with our enthusiasm, rather than let them go out with our awkwardness or dump lengthy speeches onto them! The more we show our children we're genuinely interested in their opinions and ideas, the more they will develop an ability to use them. So, the more child-led these activities can be, the more you'll all get out of them!

Principles of appreciative inquiry for families:

Conversations Worth Having, by practitioners Jackie Stavros and Cheri Torres, outlines the use of 'Appreciative Inquiry' to dramatically improve the outcome of our conversations.[25] They aim to bring about positive change in organisations and families. Conversations are the best tool we have. They build relationships, they resolve conflict and conversations help generate creative ideas.

Have you ever had a great day ruined by a conversation with someone that is full of complaint and negativity? Or had a bad day picked up by a conversation full of grace and gentleness? Some conversations are memorable because they are defining moments in a relationship as they provide insight or give direction. Conversations can shape us and change us and influence our choices. A conversation that matters can be precious. With our children, we're never too sure which conversation will become a defining teachable moment. So let's cultivate a family culture of great conversations all the time.

There are two basic dimensions for conversations that matter. The first is whether they add value (appreciate) or devalue (depreciate). **Appreciative conversations share ideas and suggest possibilities.** They acknowledge everyone's contribution, point out opportunities and respond to questions with new perspectives. Perhaps you've been part of a collaborative team that came up with a creative solution or have been publicly acknowledged for your great work? Feels good, right? A depreciative conversation, though, can belittle. It's critical, doesn't listen to others' ideas or has a domineering or complaining negative force. These conversations are exhausting and smother creativity.

The second dimension looks at conversations that are either inquiry- or statement-based. Inquiry-based questions aim to generate information. They reveal hidden ideas, deepen understanding or facilitate change. **Curiosity is at the heart of these questions.** A good questioner can make us feel valued and inspired. The motivation is key – curiosity rather than judgement or criticism. Both inquiry- and statement-based conversations can be appreciative or depreciative depending on the content. Statements will be appreciative when they add value by making positive comments or generate ideas. Destructive statements create division and negativity and hinder creativity and growth.

In our family conversations, we are seeking to add value through appreciative questions and dialogue, which are characterised by a positive direction and a good feeling! To do this, shape your family conversations by positively framing them in a way that invites engagement and produces positive outcomes. One way to do this is to name the problem then flip it – what is the positive opposite that you do want (rather than the problem you have)? What would be the desired outcome? Partly, this is like saying 'Be careful climbing that tree' rather than 'Don't climb the tree – you'll fall!' We want self-fulfilling prophecy to be working for us! Also, though, instead of approaching the problem of where the family should go on holiday (and anticipating disagreement), positive framing might say 'Let's plan our holiday so each one of us feels like it will be wonderful', and invite creative suggestions that fit everyone.

The other way is to always have an attitude of curiosity. Seek first to understand, then to be understood, and then to work together towards a solution. If you are stuck in a conflict with your child, ask them to help come to an agreement that meets both your needs. Children are more creative than us and being involved in decision making also helps them own those decisions. It could be as simple as changing the standard 'how was your day?' question to a more positive version: 'What was the best thing that happened at school today?'

The activities in this book will give your family an opportunity to try out the principles of appreciative inquiry together.

Watch out for an increase in positivity, creativity and intimacy as a result!

Part II

On the Road

Don't ask yourself what the world needs. Ask yourself what makes you come alive, then go and do that, because what the world needs is people who have come alive.

- John Eldridge, Wild at Heart

If you want to learn to love better, you should start with a friend who you hate.

- Nicki, (6)

In a Harvard University study, a massive 96 percent of parents said they wanted to raise ethical, caring children.[26] They said the development of moral character was 'very important, if not essential'. These sound like great numbers! But the study also surveyed 10,000 young people and 80 percent reported that their parents 'are more concerned about achievement or happiness than caring for others'. Only 20 percent of the youths ranked caring for others above achievement or happiness. When modelling is so important, this disconnect is a big problem. They found that simply talking about compassion is not enough. We can't just hope for the best – we need to be intentional about developing the values we care about for our children.

George Barna, head of a big research group, has studied Millennials and Gen Z for more than a decade. He has great compassion for young people. Their parents have had to deal with rapidly changing times and now life feels scary and unpredictable to their children. His research shows that only 40 percent of young adults feel hopeful about the future and only 33 percent feel 'deeply cared for by those around me'.[27]

And that was before COVID-19! This is terribly concerning if we are trying to raise people who can care for others! What they need from us is a feeling of hope, support to get there and a sense of belonging to strengthen them along the journey.

The conversations in the four relational areas will help us do just that.

CHAPTER 3

CARING ABOUT RELATIONSHIPS

Everything hinges on relationships. We are literally born to connect to people, and we've lived in family groups of various sizes forever. Our ability to cooperate distinguishes us as a species. These connections are a major source of joy and meaning in life. We have biological mechanisms in our brains that help us bond to others and stay attached to them. Nurturing environments, or the lack of them, influence the development of brain circuitry. In this way, our genes affect our behaviour. Nature and nurture interact through relationships to influence early development and well-being.

1. How are we going now?

Culturally, we're becoming increasingly individualistic: Families are becoming more mobile and less extended. Children are facing increased isolation as both parents are more likely working and kids are at home with their computers. There's less playing in the street with neighbourhood kids than when my kids were in the street with their skateboard ramps. And since our brains have still only evolved to be living in a village of about 150 people – everyone in the city is stressed.

Our whole Western society has increased its use of antidepressants and at a younger and younger age. Are we getting depressed about the state of the world – it's stuffed up and there's nothing I can do – and our lack of social connection? Or do we feel guilty, and since guilt is not a motivator, we need ways to escape these bad feelings? Our society gives us a million ways to distract ourselves or escape from any bad feelings. This means we aren't facing them.

The trouble is that in all this, we lose empathy. Not just for the human masses, but for those nearer to us. *'Oh something bad has happened to you – sorry, but I just haven't got any energy left to care for that; I have enough on my own plate!'* We get stressed and busy, we get numb to suffering, and when things get a bit overwhelming, we sit in our rooms and watch a movie. This is not good for me, or for you, or for us as a society. It's also not good for our children.

When we're stressed, we try to control rather than connect. Parenting expert Robin Grille says that when we see our children as adversaries trying to manipulate or outsmart us, who therefore need our authoritarian discipline, then we're focusing on behaviour, not connection.[28] This contributes to conflict. Truly considerate behaviour is much more likely when inspired by authentic and empathetic connections. Thus, our job is to build up our children's emotional intelligence using our own.

In summary, we are too focused on ourselves and spend too much time in isolation, which has resulted in less empathy.

2. What can we imagine would be better?

Who do you go to when you need someone who cares? Someone who accepts you, listens to you, believes in you? Powerful, isn't it?

A friend of mine was having trouble with a close girlfriend. Their conflict had come to a head, and as my friend was telling me all about it, I assumed she was about to draw a boundary and the relationship would be over. I've never forgotten my surprise at her next statement: *'I guess I will just have to love her harder.'* She believed in and supported her friend, and they remain friends many years later. I gained a new respect for the work required to love another person. I also realised the noble integrity of my friend's decision – her courageous vulnerability – and I want friends like this in my life too!

It is possible to help our children grow relationships that will last.

To imagine better relationships, think of a world where everyone has a strong sense of empathy and love. Empathy is a magic way to improve relationships. Showing empathy to someone shows we care, and it helps them progress. It grows the relationship, and it grows us by helping us understand viewpoints other than just our own. It heals conflict in this way. Essentially, conflict-mediation techniques are just empathy in action – a structured way to listen and understand one another. Building a family culture of empathy will reap huge rewards in the teenage years because it will improve communication and is a safe place to test out ideas and problems.

There are three kinds of empathy:[29]

- *Cognitive empathy* helps us understand how someone feels. Medical personnel need to maintain professional distance, but there is a danger of this leading to indifference. A friend who is a newsreader says she can't afford to feel too much about what she's reading on air. 'I might feel bad and then I have to read the next story … I'd be a mess.' It's not in any child's interest to be overcome by every sad story they come across, but neither do we want to see them sheltered and disconnected from the real world.

- *Emotional empathy* is when we really feel another's emotion. We cry when they cry. Teenagers are particularly vulnerable to this level of empathy. This 'sympathy' can be psychologically exhausting, even leading to burnout if the feelings stay with us and bring us down too. Children notice people doing it tough and can be overcome if they're given no way to respond.

- *Compassionate empathy* is when we understand and feel a person's plight, but we're also moved to help. A compassionate response is not just to cry with a grieving friend, but to help them organise the funeral. My son, as a very young boy, was moved to help the first time he saw a man living with a severe disability begging overseas. He was selling postcards, but we didn't have any money on us to buy one at the time, and my son was distraught at not being able to help. This unhappy experience became a defining moment in his compassionate development, shaping his generous empathy for life. It is at this level that we want to help build empathy in our children. It's this level that will ensure they grow emotional health, resilience and self-efficacy in the process.

We can imagine the world would be a better place with more compassionate empathy. After all, empathy guides children's moral behaviour towards others; they wouldn't want to hurt someone because they know how bad it would feel. You might experience sadness if you see someone who is sad. It's a fundamentally social response, showing that our emotions are not just narcissistic but connected to the state of other people around us. People must have empathy, especially in leadership at home, work, and in politics, where people with power must try and understand how someone without a voice, few opportunities, work prospects or money feels.

Luckily, we are seeing some changes in the right direction. Some schools are rolling out a Canadian program called the Roots of Empathy.[30] Parents come in with a baby and children have to think about the baby, name their emotions and work out how to help the baby cope with its distress. After the program, the participating children had declining rates of aggression and bullying. They have increased empathy and understanding of their own emotions.

David DeSteno at Northeastern University in the USA has shown that we can grow compassion.[31] If we can draw an association, even a trivial one, between ourselves and someone else, we make an empathetic connection. For example, if we think of a neighbour as a fan of the same local restaurant instead of as a member of a different ethnicity, our compassion for them increases.

The 'Making Caring Common' project at Harvard University also has a wealth of practical information on building empathy in children and is worth a visit.[32] For example, they have tips for modelling empathy for others, making 'kindness' a high priority and providing opportunities for children to practise, particularly outside their normal circle.

We need more of these programs to get our world to where we want it to be.

In summary, we can imagine a better world where kids are taught compassionate empathy.

3. What can we change to get there?

Help children to feel worthy of love

Do you watch TED talks?[33] Dr Brené Brown became famous when she presented her social research on vulnerability and shame.[34] It's one of the most popular TED talks of all time, partly because she makes herself vulnerable as she does it. Her research on what helps people live fulfilled and connected lives is based on thousands of interviews. She divided her sample into those people who had a strong sense of love and belonging and those who really struggled to find it. Those with a strong sense of love believed they were worthy. Brené Brown found that the only thing that keeps some people from connecting with others – from taking relational risks – is that they don't think that they are worthy of connection. Thus, one of our most crucial tasks as parents is to help our children feel worthy of love.

Brené Brown says many worthy things. She talks about having compassion for ourselves to help us be kind to others who are also imperfect, and to cultivate 'courageous vulnerability', which is acknowledging and sharing our imperfection. Courageously vulnerable people say 'sorry' or 'I love you' first. They invest without expecting payback. They help out and host visitors and keep trying and let people cry.

Embrace Conflict

A while ago I got to go back to university to study Peace and Conflict. I felt so young and groovy again! People had come from all over the world to study this course, and I'm still friends with some of them. I'll save you a lot of time and essay writing: Whether we are talking about international conflict or interpersonal, the theories about peace and conflict are the same. People of any rank are just people, and people get into conflict. That's the nature and beauty of our diversity. Two truths summarise the whole degree: **conflict is certain but it's not necessarily bad, and the best way to make it good is with communication.**

Whether it's peace talks between Israel and Palestine or mediation between a married couple, the aim is the same: get both sides to listen to the other's version of the problem. This builds an understanding of a different perspective and empathy for the other person's feelings. Mediation just sets up a structured environment for this to happen.

The trouble is when conflict arises, we're often scared of it; we all respond differently to it and we don't believe it is helpful. **But conflict dealt with well can build amazing intimacy.** When a friend comes to me to point out something I've done wrong, I can choose to get defensive and mad. Or I can appreciate that person has overcome fear to raise this issue, and that means they must love me enough to do it. We discipline our kids even though it's hard work because we love them. We might not bother with a random kid. Friends that do this for me are so relaxing to be around. I can trust that if there's a problem, they'll tell me – so I don't worry what they're thinking the rest of the time!

In a family, we can get a bit sloppy about the environment that makes conflict constructive. In fact, the family is crucial for developing our conflict resolution skills. When kids fight with their siblings, they are practising in a safe environment. Their siblings are people that will love them no matter what disagreements they have. In my marriage, we've learnt to trust that just because we disagree and it's hard and uncomfortable during a fight, we'll eventually get through it. That's what stops us from running out the door when it's hard!

We can help our kids learn to fight fairly by occasionally letting them see us resolve our disagreements and by occasionally letting them disagree with us. Conflict can be healthy if we learn to use the right tools. Learning to hone their arguments around the dinner table will help our kids express their ideas and opinions when they encounter conflict out in the world.

In her wonderful book *Families: Mine Yours Ours*, Sallie Hammond has a very helpful chapter on conflict in families.[35] It's titled 'It's not my fault!' Sallie outlines tools to give families the best chance to teach kids good conflict resolution skills. She's even made them into the acronym: CONFLICT! There's an upcoming activity for your family that revolves around them.

Grow Resilience

When I was travelling, I met an amazing girl, and she saved me from a boring job in England with an invite to travel to Greece and Turkey with her. Kate had something I hadn't worked out yet: she was comfortable with herself. It meant she didn't seem to worry so much about what people were thinking. In particular, about what she wore (a big problem for teenage girls), and this made her very attractive. Kate and I have been friends now for decades, and I still treasure her depth of wisdom and commitment to life. She brings me joy and she helps me be me.

Kate is not a churchgoer, but when I want to test out my sermon ideas, she's my favourite go-to person. She has, of course, helped with this book too! A while ago, friends of Kate's went through the unimaginable tragedy of losing a daughter. Each time I saw Kate, she'd update me on their situation. The parents were Christians and Kate could see how their faith had helped them through their daughter's illness and the sadness of her death. I remember Kate asking me at the time, 'What framework are you giving your kids to help them deal with the inevitable hardships of life?' I've also had friends lose their gorgeous teenage son to cancer and watched as their faith carried them all through. It was inspirational.

What helps some people grow in strength through hardship while others are dragged under by it? What makes some people more resilient than others? How are some people able to forgive while others harbour bitterness forever? Faith systems and psychological research can help us navigate these questions. So we'll look at some activities we can do as families to build strength in the good times to prepare us for life's inevitable hard times.

When my sons were in primary school, I worried that, for them, the inverse of 'what doesn't kill you makes you strong' was true. They'd had such a great life, maybe they would crumple when something bad happened?! Then I came across a workshop on resilience given by family psychologist Lyn Worsley. I bought her strangely titled book, *The Resilience Doughnut*.[36] The 'doughnut' is a diagram that helps show which external factors can build protective resilience. These are factors that surround and protect a child from stress or hard times. The child is the hole in the middle, and their view of themselves and their abilities is what surrounds them. I found it a helpful and hopeful tool.

Resilience is a popular topic, but less talked about is how resilience factors into relationships. The connection is circular: being more resilient helps kids be more positive with themselves and others, building better relationships, and maintaining strong relationships helps them become more resilient and able to withstand trials as they come.

Lyn Worsley quotes research that shows resilience skills can be learnt at an early age. One method is to help children become more aware of the way they explain why things happen. The idea is to move from pessimistic-thinking styles to optimistic. For example, when bad things happen, it helps to be able to see this as a temporary phase, as a specific (rather than catastrophic) situation that we can learn from, and as something outside of ourselves that we can impact. So empowering children to believe that they can make a difference to their temporary, specific adversities can help build ongoing resilience.

The International Resilience Project combined research across organisations and 30 countries.[37] They showed these factors are the same across culture and socioeconomic levels. Sadly, though, not all caregivers know how to build resilience in the children they care for, leaving them feeling helpless, sad and unloved. Edith Gotberg summarised the findings into three categories: 'I have, I am, I can'. A child may 'have' people who love them, who set limits and who keep them safe. Resilient self-worth says 'I am' likeable, respectful, responsible, hopeful. And a child may say 'I can' talk to others when I'm frightened or need to solve a problem.

All three categories are needed to build resilience.

A child may be loved (I have), but if they have no inner strength (I am), or social, interpersonal skills (I can), the child will not be resilient.

A child may have a great deal of self-esteem (I am), but if they do not know how to communicate with others or solve problems (I can), and no one to help them (I have), the child will not be resilient.

A child may be very verbal and speak well (I can), but if he or she has no empathy (I am) or does not learn from role models (I have), the child will not be resilient.[38]

Lyn Worsley shows that **resilience grows when children are exposed to experiences that help them grow an optimistic style of thinking.** The more of these, the better the outcomes. She also lists factors that cultivate resilience. I can't do justice to the seven resilience factors here: parents, skill, family, education, peer group, community and money. [39]

The *Resilience Doughnut* is based on what works practically to support this optimism. It is strengths-based, meaning we want to help children concentrate on the resilience factors that are already positive and strong for them. Not all of us have access to all the factors and not all the factors work well for each child. Worsely says we only need three external resilience factors working well for us to build resilience to manage in the world. Our job as parents is to find three that work for our child and build them up. Which three are strongest for your children? You can explore them together in the resilience conversation coming.

Improve communication skills

You can build a good family culture with emotionally healthy kids! Good family communication will see you through the challenging teen years. Communication is the foundation of everything – of building and repairing relationships. In dealing with whatever problems we'll come up against, communication skills will be what gets us through. Luckily, as we learn from psychological research, each generation of parents does a little better job of building these skills into their children's futures.

The activities in this section will help your family learn to communicate better together – in good times and bad – by focusing on someone else. These are skills that will improve every relationship you have or will have. The key to empathy is listening to another person – with your ears, your eyes, your heart and your mind. It helps us show love, heal wounds and broaden our life wisdom. Have fun practising!

Summary

To help strengthen our relationships and build compassionate empathy, our kids need to know they are worthy of love and how to build loving relationships. To do this, they'll need good communication skills and have relationships that help them cultivate resilience. Their relationships with others will not thrive if they don't first have a good relationship with themselves. And as we all know, conflict will enter any relationship, so it's best they know how to handle it.

People don't care how much you know until they know how much you care.

- Theodore Roosevelt

Life is relationships. That's all there is.

- Holly, (16)

I know my older sister loves me because she gives me all her old clothes and has to go out and buy new ones.

- Laura, (4)

CHAPTER 4

CONVERSATIONS FOR
OUR RELATIONSHIPS

Review the pre-activity notes for children at the end of the introduction before you begin the conversations. Grab notebooks and choose someone to read.

Making Good Conversation

 ## I. Where we're headed

Knowing how to get people to talk is a great way to start a conversation and to show people you're interested in them.

 ## 2. Packing our bags: what we need to know, or something to stimulate our thinking

On a long drive one day, my son asked, 'How do you have a conversation?'

I said, 'You just ask questions about the other person. Try it out on Dad – if you can get him to talk, you can get anyone to!' (He's the world's best listener so always turns the conversation away from himself!)

So my son asked, 'Hey, Dad, do you like cheese?' From that silly beginning, a half-hour conversation began, and a family joke we'll probably have for life was born. Whenever we're out with people we don't know well, someone will always ask, 'Do you like cheese?' and then we tell them the story to get a conversation started.

 ## 3. Reading the map: instructions or preparation

Choose five questions from the interview list below, write them down and choose a friend or family member to interview. You'll be surprised how much you'll discover!

4. On the road: our conversation

* What's something you find difficult to do?
* Where do you feel most comfortable?
* If you were an animal, what would you be, and why?
* How do you deal with your own anger?
* What do you most often dream about?
* When do you feel most uncomfortable?
* Under what circumstances would you tell a lie?
* What sort of place would you most like to live and why?

 # 5. Unpacking

* What did you learn that you didn't know about someone before?
* Did you enjoy answering the questions?

 # 6. Making the journey matter

Try asking your friends some of these questions this week and report back to your family!

Love Languages

 ## 1. Where we're headed

We'll be able to show love better to the people we care about by learning to speak their love languages as described in a series of famous books by counsellor Gary Chapman.[40]

 ## 2. Packing our bags: what we need to know, or something to stimulate our thinking

On this trip, we will learn *the five love languages*. I never really understood my dad. I only lived with him until I was eight, then we lived with Mum, and for a long time Dad lived overseas and we only saw him once a year. He's not a very talkative guy – he's an action man. He took us horse-riding and ice-skating and camping and bushwalking and skiing. I found out when I grew up that he was shy as a kid. I found it hard to talk to him, and I found it hard to figure out if he really liked me. Sounds weird – he thinks it's weird – but that's how I felt.

Dad remarried a lady who was really good at talking. She would spend a whole day catching up on my life and its little stories. She taught me about D&Ms – deep and meaningful conversations – about feelings and relationship issues. It wasn't just a girl thing – she taught her sons too. I felt like she loved me, and we connected more than I could with my dad.

Then one day I read a book by an experienced counsellor. Gary Chapman's book *The Five Love Languages* changed my life! The book has helped people all over the world learn to love their families better. He noticed that different people like to give and show love in different ways.

Some of us need words, some a hug or a gift, some like help and some need to spend time with their loved ones. The trouble is, sometimes people just miss connecting with each other because they're not seeing love in the same way. Almost like they're speaking another language!

I realised that Dad and I just didn't talk the same love language. I needed words, and he wasn't very fluent in that love language. He was showing me he loved me in other ways, and I had missed it. It really helped to know that.

3. Reading the map: instructions or preparation

As I explain each of the five love languages, see if you can work out which language each person in your family prefers to speak. Stop and talk about each one as you go. It might be harder for younger kids, but that's OK because we all need all of them anyway, we just have different preferences!

Or: there are quizzes for adults, teens and 9 - 12 year old's at https://www.5lovelanguages.com/quizzes/

4. On the road: our conversation

WORDS

Some people think words are very important. They might give compliments, might get very upset at criticism, they might listen well or they write great cards.

To speak their love language, you can tell them you love them, thank them, have a great conversation, write them a note or find out what their dreams are and encourage them!

'I know my parents love me because they are always interested in hearing about my day or my life.'

TIME

Some people like to spend time together – they just love knowing they have your undivided attention. The trick is to do something with them that they like to do – playing monopoly, kicking a ball, doing a puzzle – whatever.

To speak this language, find out what activities they like to do and do it with them!

'I know my dad loves me because he always comes to my games and helps me practise.'

GIFTS

I bet you know someone who is great at remembering your birthday and often gives you nice gifts. Or maybe they get very sad if someone forgets theirs. Some people feel really loved when they're given a gift because it means someone was thinking about them.

If you love someone who loves gifts, keep a list of things they like and get more creative and generous about giving them these things, or even encouraging others too.

'When I want to know what to get my son for his birthday I ask his girlfriend. She keeps a list all year when he says he likes something.'

HELPING

Does Mum or Dad get especially happy when someone helps them with chores around the house? Does someone make your favourite cake or help clean your room when you're feeling down? Maybe helping is their love language. If so, whenever you can, find a little way to help them; they will feel loved by you!

You could ask them to write a list of what they find helpful. It's much nicer helping someone as a gift of love than if it's just a chore!

'Words don't mean much to me, but I'm so grateful when someone washes up for me.'

TOUCH

Have you noticed how some people are more touchy-feely-cuddly-affectionate than others? Some people might touch your arm when they say hello or even give you a big bear hug! All people need hugs, but if it's your love language, you need them even more than others!

If someone you love might speak this language, then things like a touch on the shoulder when they're feeling sad, a kiss to say thank you or a hug goodnight will be very clear messages of love.

'Oh I love your hugs – it feels like you really mean it!'

5. Unpacking

* How did you feel hearing other people have different ways of seeing love? Did it bring an experience to mind?
* Check whether anyone is feeling sad or disappointed right now.
* Let everyone suggest one way they would feel more loved this week.

 ## 6. Making the journey matter

* This is your chance to learn new love languages. Remember, it's not about you – it's about learning to love other people the way they like it or might best 'hear' it.
* Pick something new to try out on your family this week.
* You could put all your names in a hat and pick one each to be your secret buddy this week to test out your new skills on!

Being a Great Friend

 ## 1. Where we're headed

Friends make life better, so we want to learn to be a great friend.

 ## 2. Packing our bags: what we need to know, or something to stimulate our thinking

I asked some of my young students for friendship advice and they suggested:

* Don't talk behind people's backs
* Be nice to everyone
* If you don't have anything nice to say, don't say anything
* Consider other's feelings
* Think before you act
* Never, ever gossip

Sarah's story:

> "One day at high school, my friends went off without me. When I went after them, they said, 'We don't want you in our group anymore. You think you're too good!'
>
> I was devastated. I thought, That's a lie. I do not! but I didn't say anything. Then I realised it didn't matter if it was true or not, because if I gave them that impression, I was going to lose friends, so I needed to change.
>
> I discovered something easy you can do to build people up. You just have to give people attention. It's like a gift. Treat them like they matter. It works with old people, disabled people, super-popular people; it even works with dogs. And when you do that, you're living the truth because they do matter."

3. Reading the map: instructions or preparation

That's good advice. So how do we give people attention without just changing ourselves for others?

To prepare for the conversation, think of a time you've been really helped by a friend or really enjoyed their company.

What qualities do you think make a good friend? For example, *A good friend is .... trustworthy, loving, caring, patient, listens, fun, encouraging, helpful ...*

4. On the road: our conversation

Write a job description for your perfect friend here ...

Wanted: *Perfect Friend*

Essential Qualities: _____

Desirable Qualities: _____

Undesirable Qualities: _____

How do you fit this description? Are you a good friend?

Ask everyone to describe a good friend and say why they like them.

5. Unpacking

* Each person can come up with something they'd like to work on this week to be a better friend.
* Check whether this topic has made anyone a little sad. Maybe you've experienced some undesirable friendship qualities. These can help us decide what we don't want to be like! Sometimes though, we might realise a friend is just not a good friend to us. What do we do then?

6. Making the journey matter

* Write down something specific you will do for a friend this week.
* Write how you'll try to be a better friend yourself.

Listening Well

 ## 1. Where we're headed

The average person will listen for 17 seconds before interrupting. We're going to improve that average!

 ## 2. Packing our bags: what we need to know, or something to stimulate our thinking

When I was studying psychology, I did the 'Lifeline' telephone counselling training and worked on the phones for a while. People needing a 'lifeline' rang up for someone to talk to them. The listener's job was to help the caller find hope that they could come up with solutions to their problems – to listen, not talk. There's now a Kids Helpline too.

There were lots of older mums in the training course. As a young adult, I remember the strong language used to tell these volunteer women that now that their own children had left home, they could not offer their motherly advice to people calling for counselling! Listening, not speaking, was to be the order of the day.

Listening is a way to show care – and it's rare. It needs more than just ears, it needs brain and heart too. Being listened to helps us verbally process our thoughts, and it's at the heart of all counselling and conflict resolution. So, it's pretty important!

 ## 3. Reading the map: instructions or preparation

To prepare for the activity, think of a time you were feeling stressed about a problem and went to someone to talk.

How did you feel when they listened?

How did you feel if they told you what you *should* do?

---

4. On the road: our conversation

Take this quiz: How well do I listen?

1. When I'm listening on the phone, I:
   a) sometimes take notes to remember what's been said
   b) often draw on the pad next to the phone
   c) watch TV at the same time so I don't get bored

2. When one of my friends tells me about a problem they're having, I:
   a) ask what they've tried so far
   b) tell them what they should do to fix it
   c) tell them what happened to me last night

3. When someone in my family asks me to help them I:
   a) come running straight away
   b) just keep doing what I'm doing
   c) yell out, 'it's not my turn!'

4. If someone is angry at me, I say:
   a) 'I'm sorry you're so angry. Tell me what's wrong.'
   b) 'it's not my fault.'
   c) 'get lost; you're such a jerk.'

5. If a teacher asks me to listen to some instructions, I:
   a) put down my pen and look at them
   b) know I can ask someone what they said later
   c) keep talking, not interested

6. When someone in my family bursts into tears, I:
   a) hug them and ask 'What's wrong?'
   b) leave the room to give them some privacy
   c) tell them to stop being such a cry baby

7. If someone is talking to me, I:
   a) look at them and concentrate
   b) sometimes get distracted
   c) think about what I'm going to say next

How to Score:

For every a) you chose, count 3 points

For every b) you chose, count 1 point

For every c) you chose, sorry, <u>deduct</u> one point!

If you scored …

<7   Oh, so that's why no one seems to like me'

8–14   You may wonder why you don't have great friends

15–20 You are a good friend and probably want to be an even better listener

21   Are you available to teach a friendship class next week? People could learn a lot from you!

 # 5. Unpacking

* How did you go? Ask your family how well they feel listened to.
* Do some people in your family talk more than others?
* Why do you think listening is important?

At home, which of these is worse? How does your house work? What might you change?
a) no one talks at all; there's just icy silence
b) everyone talks, but it's at the top of their lungs
c) everyone talks; no one listens

 # 6. Making the journey matter

* How many mouths do we have? How many ears. Try using them in that ratio.
* Find out something new about someone in your family this week.

Paying Attention

 ## 1. Where we're headed

We're going to practise our listening skills together so we can get better at showing friends and family we care about them.

 ## 2. Packing our bags: what we need to know, or something to stimulate our thinking

There's a game called, strangely, 'Ungame' that was invented by a lady named Rhea Zakich. Rhea had a full life and loved to talk and teach, but she had throat surgery and had to be silent for several months, not knowing if she would ever speak again! While she was quiet, she realised her family didn't actually listen to each other, especially about their feelings and deeper thoughts. She wrote down questions she wished people would ask and the questions she couldn't ask out loud. They became a game played by millions of people!

Becoming a good listener will help in every area of our lives. We'll show people we care and have better relationships, but we'll also learn more about people and about the world!

 ## 3. Reading the map: instructions or preparation

Listening is something we can learn and all new skills need practise. We're going to practise listening by taking turns answering some 'Ungame' questions.

Each speaker can choose the question they'd like to answer (or put them all in a hat). When someone else is speaking, you need to be completely silent until the speaker finishes.

When they finish speaking, you can ask a follow-up question. Try to talk for at least a minute.

Do as many rounds as you like.

4. On the road: our conversation

* What kind of reading do you enjoy and why?
* Talk about a special wish you have.
* How does music affect your life?
* What is your favourite time of day and why?
* Describe something you like to do that seems out of the ordinary.
* Tell about a special gift you once received.
* What is one thing you could do to improve your life?
* Talk about a time when you felt left out.
* Talk about taking risks.
* What do you find beautiful?
* What would you do if you could only be connected to the internet for one hour each week?

5. Unpacking

* Talk about how it felt to have everyone listening to you.
* Do you think you are good at listening in your family?

6. Making the journey matter

How will you practise listening this week? It's great to do this when you have people over for dinner.

Another conversation-starting game to play with friends is 'Big Talk' (as opposed to small talk).

Find it at https://www.makebigtalk.com/.

Caring by Listening

 ## 1. Where we're headed

To acquire advanced listening skills, which means showing we've heard and understood, and we are looking for their emotions.

 ## 2. Packing our bags: what we need to know, or something to stimulate our thinking

Each week in my Lifeline course, we had to practise in groups of three. One person would speak, one would listen, and one would observe.

* The speaker was given a little role play – to pretend they were in a difficult situation.
* The listener would have to ask questions after they spoke to show they were interested. To show they understood and help the person work out what feeling was underlying their story, they might also confirm the speaker's thoughts and feelings (e.g., 'It sounds like you feel very angry about what happened.'). Naming our feelings really helps us understand and manage them.
* The observer would then say how well the listener had done!

 ## 3. Reading the map: instructions or preparation

It would be great if each person had a chance to try out each of the three roles, but at least try the listening triplets once or twice in your family group. Of course if there's only two of you, you can take time to reflect anyway.

4. On the road: our conversation

* The speaker can choose a story in their mind that shows a particular feeling. Think of a time you felt angry or sad or disappointed or joyful or loved or excited. Or make up something wild!
* Set a one-minute timer.
* The listener should try to resay what the speaker has said in a short sentence and figure out what emotion they are feeling.
* The observer can add to the listener's responses.
* Swap and try again!

 ## 5. Unpacking

* How often does someone listen like this to you in real life?
* How did it feel to be the listener or observer? Was it hard work?

 ## 6. Making the journey matter

Who could you try out your new skills on this week? You could practise again as a family.

Coping When You've Made a Mistake

1. Where we're headed

Knowing what to do when you've done something wrong will help you mend relationships with your family and friends and help you feel better about yourself.

2. Packing our bags: what we need to know, or something to stimulate our thinking

Justin is in year 8 and the youngest in his family of four kids, so he has always been the king of hand-me-downs. But an older friend just gave him a guitar. His very own.

Luke, four years older, also plays guitar and started borrowing Justin's guitar without asking. This went on for a while and caused heaps of tension.

Finally, Justin decided to lock the guitar to a stand in his room. Problem solved? No way. Luke was furious and pulled at the guitar and suddenly broke the whole neck off. When he realised what he'd done, he was horrified.

When we do something wrong, our first instincts are to hide in shame or shift the blame to someone or something else. We can even try to hurt ourselves as punishment because we are so angry with ourselves. But none of these solve the problem or heal the relationship.

Justin wasn't home yet, so Luke went to talk to his dad in a panic. His dad gave Luke a three-step plan.

1. **Admit**: Admit that you did something wrong. Don't get angry. (Justin had a right to be angry, but Luke didn't, and it would only make things worse).

2. **Apologise:** Give a sincere apology. Half-hearted 'sorry's just make the wronged person feel worse. How can you show you mean it?

3. **Amend:** Quickly offer to find a way to fix what's happened. Show that you are willing to make up for what you have done.

 ## 3. Reading the map: instructions or preparation

The thing about this story is that it wasn't about a guitar at all. Every time Luke took the guitar, Justin had felt that his brother didn't care about his feelings, that he wasn't important or respected. This was especially hard since he was the youngest, but everyone wants to feel loved and important in their family.

Knowing this information, why do you think the three-step plan was effective?

When Luke apologised, Justin saw that his brother did care about him (because Luke felt so bad!), and that was more important than the guitar (which they fixed). The apology was the beginning of a much better relationship between the brothers. All the old tension went away!

This just goes to show that when we have courage to do the right thing, great things can even come out of bad situations.

 ## 4. On the road: our conversation

* Share a time you've done something wrong and how you felt about it.
* How could you have applied the three-step plan to that time? Could you try saying:
  1. I did something…
  2. I'm sorry that I…
  3. I want to put it right…
* Would this plan work in your family?

5. Unpacking

We all make mistakes sometimes. Remembering what that feels like helps us forgive people when they mess up. Is the courage required worth it?

If Justin had refused to accept Luke's apology, the brothers would still be at war. Worse though, Justin would still feel terrible about himself – unloved and disrespected in his family. Hanging on to your anger is really bad for you! The other person often doesn't even know (or care) so you're just hurting yourself. **Forgiving someone is one of the best things you can ever do. It shows real strength!**

 # 6. Making the journey matter

Think of your own example of when someone's done the wrong thing. How would the three-step plan help?

It's going to be tricky to remember, but next time you make a mistake, see if you can try out the three-step plan.

How to Find Forgiveness

 1. Where we're headed

Learning to forgive is powerful for the person we forgive, but is especially important for healing ourselves.

Warning: this is a pretty intense story. There's quite a lot to this topic and sometimes forgiving will be easier than others. It's not talked about much as a method for resolving conflict in Hollywood – action revenge scenarios are much more exciting! But learning to forgive will make our lives better.

 2. Packing our bags: what we need to know, or something to stimulate our thinking

My sister Jenny and I were best friends as kids. I guess this was partly because when the adults in our lives were having troubles – fighting, moving, remarrying – we always had each other. We shared a bedroom until I was 16, and we would chat and laugh every night.

We were very different people, though, and when I moved into my own room, we started to drift apart. Without our nightly catch-ups, we stopped understanding each other so well. Jenny was bolder and would argue loudly with our stepfather. She also started being mean to me, and we argued too.

By the time she got expelled from school at 17 and thrown out of home at 19, we were no longer close. After travelling overseas for many months, I rang home one afternoon, and I discovered my only sister had been killed by a drunk driver that very day.

This was pretty terrible. But do you know what the very worst thing was? I could never fix our relationship. I could never say 'I forgive you for being mean to me.' I'm sure if she was alive now we would be close again – but we never can.

When I hear about brothers and sisters now who argue and stop talking to each other, I want to tell them this story. This very bad thing that has happened to me has given me some wisdom I think. I will never, never give up on my only brother. I will always fix problems in my family or friendships as quickly as possible. I will appreciate people, even when they are different from me. I will also never drink too much alcohol and drive!

I'm not really perfect at forgiveness, but my experience helps me to choose how to live. It also makes me a good friend when someone loses someone they love – I know what it's like.

A while after Jenny died, I visited her grave, and I cried and told her that I forgave her, that I missed her and would rather she was here and mean to me than not here at all. It didn't bring her back, but it helped me to be stronger to cope with it.

 ## 3. Reading the map: instructions or preparation

Scientific studies have shown there are many benefits of forgiving.[41] One of the leading methods for forgiving is REACH:

R – recall the hurt, feel the feelings, but also remember when we've messed up

E – empathise with what the person was trying to do (even if they messed up badly and it's hard).

A- give an 'altruistic' (unselfish) gift of forgiveness. It might help to be grateful for the times we've been forgiven.

C- commit to telling someone else that you need to do some forgiving – this might not be the forgiven person.

H- hold on to it – become a forgiving person over time.

4. On the road: our conversation

Talk together in your family about:

* times you have or haven't been forgiven
* times you have or haven't forgiven others
* how the REACH method might have helped
* or what parts might be hard for you

> 'I believe exposing students to models of healthy forgiveness and then having them analyze and reflect on the how's and why's that person came to forgive, gives them lifelong tools that transcend any academic lesson I could possibly teach them. To learn to forgive authentically and well is an essential life skill that is not attained by osmosis and, yet, if learned guarantees a happier, more fulfilled life.'
>
> —*Ginger Lewis, Teacher*

Do you think forgiving can make you happier? (Hint: or how might not forgiving affect you?)

 # 5. Unpacking

* How do you feel about this topic? What emotions were involved?
* Was it hard to talk about? Did you disagree?

Forgiving is complex. Anger is normal. Forgiving doesn't mean condoning bad behaviour, and it also might not mean things are ever the same. The trick is to realise the long-term anger and bitterness from not forgiving is worse. It's worth the act of courage to stretch yourself through the pain to forgive to set yourself free.

6. Making the journey matter

There's a lot more to think about here. Perhaps over dinner sometimes you could mention what you forgave this week. Perhaps there's a letter you could write to show someone you forgive them?

For more information about the REACH method of forgiving, you could download a free workbook on it from a leading psychologist at https://evworthington.squarespace.com/diy-workbooks.[42]

Another great resource is The Forgiveness Project.[43] It's full of stories of forgiveness, and they have free materials that schools or families can use. Probably best for older families, though.

Fighting Fair

 ## 1. Where we're headed

Learning some skills to resolve conflict well.

 ## 2. Packing our bags: what we need to know, or something to stimulate our thinking

I heard about a great method a single mum with four kids had. When the children came to her fighting or with a grievance, she asked them to write the problem down (or draw it) with everyone's perspective. She had a special 'inbox' for them to put it in. She told them she'd review the problem later. Nearly always, the act of writing and being heard calmed the situation down or even resolved it.

Communication is the best tool we have for resolving conflict. And conflict is an inevitable part of life when we have such a diverse range of people and preferences. In fact, conflict can be a good thing. It can deepen the trust and intimacy of our relationships as we learn that we will be heard and understood, and that conflict won't ruin us.

 ## 3. Reading the map: instructions or preparation

In her wonderful book *Families: Mine Yours Ours*, Sallie Hammond has a very helpful chapter on conflict in families titled 'It's not my fault!' She's built the tools to give families the best chance to teach kids good conflict resolution skills into an acronym CONFLICT!

C – stay CALM and be ready to COMPROMISE: build a habit of not yelling and understand you may need to negotiate.

O – take OPPORTUNITIES to be positive: When you say something affirming like 'That's a good point; I hadn't thought about it that way' (rather than being defensive), you actually defuse the anger and you can start working together on the problem.

N – 'never' and 'always' are no-nos: extreme language and exaggeration just inflame conflict. Remember how it feels when someone says to you, 'You always let me down, you're never on my side.' It's clearly not true so not helpful.

F – FORGIVE or ask for forgiveness if necessary: Focus on behaviour that gives hope. For example, 'I'm sorry I shouted at you. Can we try talking about this again?' Owning our own contribution to the problem is great role modelling and a great way through conflict.

L – LISTEN to the problem first and LOOK for creative solutions: Ask, 'what happened?' rather than 'who started it?' Then ask, 'What do you think that was like for the other person?' to help build empathy about the other person's perspective.

I – I STATEMENTS don't blame or demand the other person changes: 'I feel (emotion) when you (behaviour)' keeps us from flaring up and blaming a person. It requires us to understand ourselves and be clear about our needs.

C – use CONCISE statements, not long lectures: Have the family discussion **before** a conflict to build family values and boundaries. For example, 'In this family we don't walk out on a fight, we don't hit, we don't call people names.'

T – TAKE A BREAK: If it's getting heated, it's often very wise to wait until intense emotion has passed to have structured conflict resolution conversations. Feel free to say this out loud and agree upon it at the time.

I'd also add **S** – SAY A PRAYER. Conflict is hard, but it's worth working on and getting all the help you can!

 ## 4. On the road: our conversation

* Try this process out with your family now. Start with a small problem or issue that is recent but maybe not current (too scary).

* Let each person share how they felt about the issue and then let someone try to restate it to be sure you've all understood.

* Next, brainstorm ways forward: How could you have handled it differently? Is there a new family rule we should make to help in the future? How did it feel to have your point of view heard?
* Once you've agreed on a solution – celebrate this impressive achievement!

 ## 5. Unpacking

* Do different people in your family like conflict more than others? Do those people usually win? Is that fair? Talk about how conflict makes you feel, so everyone knows what it's like for you.
* Bullying is connected here too. What do you think? Does your school have an anti-bullying strategy?

 ## 6. Making the journey matter

Before you judge anyone, pretend to **step into their shoes**. Imagine what life looks like from their point of view. Ask yourself, '**How would that make them feel?**' Not sure? How would it make **you** feel? You'll go a long way in your relationships with people if you can develop empathy by simply doing this.

Resilience Training –
Getting Through Hard Times

 ## 1. Where we're headed

To find ways that work for us to strengthen our resilience – our ability to bounce back and cope when bad things happen.

 ## 2. Packing our bags: what we need to know, or something to stimulate our thinking

We can learn skills to help us grow resilience, and the most helpful ones are thinking styles.[44] Optimistic-thinking habits are the most popular. People who think pessimistically, think they're stuck with bad experiences – they can't change them. They think they are somehow at fault and don't have much hope.

On the other hand, with optimistic thinkers, when bad things happen, they see them as temporary situations they can learn from. They realise bad things are caused by factors outside themselves, so they can work around them.

The good news is that when good things happen and you think optimistically, you see these things as dependable and a sign that things are going well. You know that your work makes a difference.

So pessimism makes us avoid new experiences and give up easily, but optimism keeps us trying new things until we find success.

3. Reading the map:
instructions or preparation

Research has found there are seven key areas that can increase our resilience. It's helpful to know that we don't need all seven – strength in three is enough to live well in the world. So we should focus on our three best ones.

1. Warm, open communication with parents who care.
2. Skill in a task, hobby or sport gained by trying hard and being supported.
3. Ability to participate and contribute to a wider family network, giving a sense of identity and belonging.
4. Supportive teachers and schools that encourage involvement and ownership.
5. An accepting friend or peer group that supports diversity and loyalty.
6. A community group that values children (church, sports club, library ...)
7. Understanding of the value of money – does chores, saves, raises funds, works.

4. On the road:
our conversation

* Help each family member work out whether their thinking style is more optimistic or pessimistic. Give each other suggestions for increasing optimistic thinking.
* Talk about each of the seven ways we get resilience. Let each person pick their top three.
* Take turns talking about an example of how you've managed something hard because of one of these factors.
* Think about how you could make one of them even stronger.

5. Unpacking

* Are you happy with your current levels of resilience?
* Are there any plans you'd like to make as a family to strengthen some of the resilience factors?

Hopefully, these conversations are helping with number 1!

6. Making the journey matter

Next time someone in your family is finding something hard, stop and talk about ways to think optimistically about the problem. Talk about which of the seven ways might be used to strengthen and support them through their hard time.

You can learn more here: https://www.theresiliencedoughnut.com. au/.

CHAPTER 5

CARING ABOUT CULTURE

When my boys were young, we'd travel to visit extended family during school holidays. Their cousins were allowed to watch mature movies much younger than I'd let my boys. It drove me crazy! One of my sons still had nightmares years later! Do you remember the first time you went to another house and noticed that different families operate differently? Or the first time you visited a country quite distinct from your own? We don't notice our family culture until we can compare it or until we end up in counselling!

As for the culture of our society, it has changed a lot since we were kids. Our fast-changing culture is affecting our children and that's hard to keep up with. Unless we stop to notice, it's hard to counter it.

1. How are we going now?

Wealth and consumerism

Associate Professor Paul Piff has studied the effect of our wealth for a decade now. He's found it makes us less compassionate, less generous, less ethical and more entitled. Luckily, he also has some suggestions about what we can do to counteract it, which we'll look at later. [45]

Consumerism feeds on these effects, encouraging constant discontent so we'll focus on our own 'wants' first. I'm concerned about the development of children in this environment. While children are born with a strong sense of justice and generosity, companies target children at very young ages to build them into self-focused consumers. This then causes children to exploit their pester power, and since parents just want their children to be happy, they give in. Happiness, though, is a byproduct of meaningful relationships and purpose in life, not more stuff. Our kids will become mistaken about this unless we are intentional in raising their awareness of this pervasive force in our culture.

A report commissioned by The Consumed Campaign in Australia in 2019 showed 80 percent of Australians believed people consume much more than they need.[46] The results showed that higher levels of consumption were not helpful. They meant higher daily stress, frustration and anxiety, and less daily happiness, hope and contentment.

They also found a disconnect between belief and behaviour in consumers. More than half wanted to change their buying habits. More than half thought it was very important to ensure the goods they buy were made by workers who were paid fair wages. But only a third thought it likely they *could* change their spending habits, and only 9 percent recently chose *not* to buy an unethical item. Our consumer culture has come to value economic growth over all else, even above ethics!

But by valuing economic growth, we then have the grass-is-always-greener-on-the-other-side mentality. Someone will always have more wealth than us. An interesting fact of human nature is 'relative deprivation'. **Most people are happier making $50,000 when those around them make $40,000 than they are making $60,000 when those around them make $70,000.** It skews how content we are with what we have. It affects how generous we think we can be. People tend to be happy if they are all in the same boat, but relative deprivation kicks in if we think others have much more than we do. With TV and the internet showing us lifestyles of the rich and famous every day, relative deprivation is now the norm. We can all see the gap between rich and poor, or enough and more than enough – and its social consequences.

Research on this inequality, described in *The Spirit Level: Why more equal societies almost always do better*, shows us the cost of this.[47] When income differences between rich and poor are smaller, the quality of general social relationships is better. Unequal societies were found to be less trusting, less hospitable, more unfriendly and even more violent. The vast amount of evidence collected has made an obvious link between income inequality and social dysfunction.

In fact, lack of social cohesion seemed to provide the causal link between income inequality and homicide rates. One measure of social cohesion is trust. But in unequal societies, people believe most people would try to take advantage of you if they got the chance. **Our kids are growing up with less social cohesion than we had, and an unrealistic belief that they are not well off enough.** Our focus on economic growth means that our children are growing up in a world where they will never feel they have 'enough'.

And if relative deprivation and lack of social cohesion aren't enough, our kids are also growing up in a society with economically driven politics. I was about to write that this book is not about politics. But politics is broader than what it has devolved into. Politics includes the ethics of government, peace and safety, and the improvement of rights and morals. There's a pretty decent overlap with raising kids who care here. Two professors of public health have written that our dominant forms of politics have made us sick.[48] Studies of health and well-being across Britain, Europe and the United States show that our economically driven politics have had a massively detrimental effect on the health of ordinary people. They looked at obesity, stress, austerity and inequality. Epidemics since the 1980s have fallen disproportionately on the poorest and most vulnerable. This has certainly been true in COVID-19 and we are still discovering the effects around the world. If we are becoming a society of people who don't care, then we're going to need to raise a whole generation of children who do care to reverse this trend. To do that, we'll need to understand a bit about the political forces acting upon us and the problem with wealth.

Wealth insulates people from the consequences of their actions. It reduces their need for social connections and fuels feelings of entitlement.[49] I've felt that entitlement myself. I remember visiting a very poor Indonesian village where we were supporting some development projects. We watched as our children played soccer with the village kids and heard wonderful stories about how the women had been helped to form a savings co-op (they were helping each other to grow small and sustainable businesses). When it was time to go, I climbed into the hire car and looked through the tinted window at the mass of kids clamouring around us outside. As the delicious air-con kicked in, I'll never forget the visceral feeling I had that this was where I belonged – in the cool and comfy car.

I was horrified at what a princess I'd become. Most of us born in Australia (or any rich country) take our luck for granted. We convince ourselves that we deserve what we've achieved with our free schooling and top-notch health care. Recently, I was frustrated that I had to pay a cleaner the same hourly rate that I was earning at a not-for-profit, until I realised that she has to pay the same amount for a bottle of milk as I do! It's this very ferocious sense of entitlement that stops us from having compassion for others with less. Others who, by an accident of birth, have life a lot tougher.

This is a problem because when we come across someone doing it tough who could use a bit of care, our response is clouded by our entitlement. We may feel guilt, but this isn't helpful as it's a de-motivating emotion and requires a defence mechanism distraction to deal with it. We may be paralysed by too many statistics about starving children in Africa (Stalin said 1 death is a tragedy, 1,000 a statistic ... do we want to be like him?) or we may just feel numb. If you always have enough to eat, it can be hard to understand the shouts of people whose stomachs are always grumbling from hunger. Or we may be numbed by the sheer fact that we can't do anything about it – we're overwhelmed and need to distract ourselves from our discomfort. After all, material deprivation is not the dominant feature of life in Australia, affluence is – and if we don't see that, we won't care for the poor. **So, to tackle the problem of poverty, we must also tackle the problem of affluence.**

And we need to help our children recognise that they are affluent in many ways, even if they aren't 'rich' by Western society standards. Once, teaching a class of twelve-year-old students, I asked the kids to stand along a continuum diagonally across the classroom. One end if you were rich, one if you were poor, and spread anywhere along the middle. We then spent a couple of weeks getting to know a group of children in Kenya. These children were learning to educate their villages about small but profound health issues. One of our activities describes the play these students made up for the school. Some acted parts of the Kenyan children and some as themselves, each describing aspects of their lives. The contrast was powerful. When I asked the students to stand along the continuum again at the end of the unit, they were all bunched up at the 'rich' end. It's healthy to have a realistic understanding of how well off we are, as it challenges our expectations for needing 'more'. There's a conversation about this in 'The World' section.

Clearly, we need to teach our kids to recognise their privilege and wealth and to be a smart and measured consumer. If we don't teach them, society will encourage them how to be an inappropriate shopper – going for fast and shiny over ethical. There's a harrowing documentary about the Commercialization of Childhood. [50] A smiling marketer says, *'They are tomorrow's adult consumers, so start talking with them now, build that relationship when they're younger, and you've got them as an adult.'* Marketing targeted specifically to children is big business.

The risk is that this leads children to view consumption as a primary form of self-expression. It becomes a means through which they can construct their identity. As this happens, children begin to define themselves by what they consume, rather than by who they are. Advertising shapes identity and sense of self. 'Buy this object and you'll be saved ... trust in us and buy now.' Products become tools for the appropriation of larger ideas and values.

Figures on just how many advertisements kids are exposed to vary, but if you add in websites, product placements and cross-promotions, children are pretty much marketed to all day. **The problem with this is that young children view advertising as informative rather than persuasive, so it's absorbed easily.** Teenagers are especially vulnerable, as they're so concerned with looking cool and belonging. Modern life offers a sensory avalanche, which some worry dulls our senses, while at the same time increases a young person's 'pester power'. Children between the ages of two and six who view more television advertising request products more.

Consumerism is an inescapable part of our children's lives. The good news is that they can grow faculties to be critical of it. Between the ages of 6 and 11, children begin to develop the ability to think sceptically about advertising. The products that zero in on their age group, though, are harder to resist. Companies spend an extraordinary amount of money on focus groups and experts to understand the psychology of our young people. They know they have more and more buying power. Big brands work out what they want young people to want before they even realise they want it.

And because the pleasure centre of our brain gets activated when we buy or get something we don't need, the kids will want what the big brands are saying they need. This is also why adults buy unnecessary items. The brain's very good at letting us know the rush we get when we want something and how easily it can be repeated. The main chemical involved is dopamine. When we do something that's pleasurable, the brain's reward centre is flooded with dopamine and memories are laid for the future. The brain registers all pleasures in the same way, whether it's a drug, going up a level in an online game, a sexual encounter, a satisfying meal, or shopping. Instead of remembering the 99 times shopping was not pleasurable, people remember the first time it was. Repeated exposure to behaviour also drives us towards wanting it more, and so it is for retail therapy.[51]

Expert parenting author Steve Biddulph talks about materialism too. He points out that our rushed society has less time for affection, and young people may be using porn to fill their needs for closeness and loving relationships. Biddulph thinks both low-income and high-income children are at risk of being neglected.[52] Consumer goods and food have replaced intimacy in our lives. Advertising teaches us all to evaluate ourselves by our looks. **Unless we are intentional about teaching values – like kindness, creativity, patience,**

loyalty and generosity – then we'll have nothing to offer our children apart from our money.

I've asked primary school students to imagine the world was a school playground. I asked them what they would like it to be like. They said kids should have equal access to play equipment, play fair and be happy. We all know they have a very good barometer for fairness! This is another key ingredient to generosity, and then to social justice in general.

Kids are all or nothing characters. They can be so black and white about things. [My son] says, 'Well why don't those kids have enough food?' They see what's illogical. We fuzz up the reality in a way. They see and feel the bleakness. – Kate

Children have a beautiful ability to see through complexity with their hearts. Adults complicate reasons for giving. And the richer we are, the less likely we are to make donations. The Chronicle of Philanthropy compared charitable giving in America before and after the Global Financial Crisis. Those who earned less than $100,000 a year increased their giving. In contrast, those earning more decreased their giving – and decreased it more the richer they were![53]

The pressure to consume leads to busyness racing after money, which increases wealth, which decreases empathy, mental health and ethics, which grows spiritual poverty, which is more vulnerable to the pressures of … **consumerism!**

And it isn't just consumerism that is the problem. Affluence itself can cause issues. Wealthy children were generally presumed to be at low risk of psychological unwellness. As early as 2005 though, academic research was researching their pressures too.[54] One study found problems in several domains: substance use, anxiety and depression. They found two sets of potential causes: pressure to achieve and isolation from being home alone while parents were at work. Social media and general upward mobility discourage kids from being 'ordinary'. Kids are home with devices rather than playing with kids in their neighbourhoods. It seems likely that there are connections between our fast-paced, high-pressure culture, and the increase in mental health issues amongst all of us – including our children. These pressures have only increased since the early study, as have the depression statistics. A more recent study also found adolescents from affluent families experienced high pressure to achieve, excessive parental criticism and perfectionism. Substance abuse was their main coping mechanism.[55]

Technology

My son says we've reached the age of science fiction – we are all walking cyborgs, half-human, half-robot. He's referring, of course, to the pocket-sized (now wrist-sized!) computers that are constantly attached to our bodies. I'm pretty sure we're all aware of the size of this problem now.

Recently, Dr Kristy Goodwin dispensed practical wisdom about this on the podcast *Parental as Anything*. She wrote the book *Raising Your Child in a Digital World: Finding a healthy balance of time online without techno tantrums and conflict.*[56] New research was showing that by the time a child reached eight years old, they'd have spent one whole year of their life with a digital device! The main concerns were the missed opportunities for physical play and interpersonal interaction – and the threat of internet pornography. Kids reported that it's harder to avoid porn now than find it – it finds them.

A great book to enhance this discussion is *Families in the Digital Age* by journalist and mum Toni Hassan.[57] It has plenty of practical suggestions for parents and families trying to negotiate the challenge of technology. Toni is concerned that while children are still developing their sense of self, social media holds them accountable as if they were adults. Since kids have a strong need to connect and belong (as we all do), they turn to social media to help them do that. But it allows no space to learn without the possibility of serious consequences. On top of that, social media is a technology connection rather than a real connection. This constant connection to technology causes several problems: We become easily distracted and develop disconnection anxiety (FOMO – fear of missing out). We experience a tyranny of the urgent, and a shrinkage of space for other things in our lives. Toni says neuroscience research shows that our constant e-multi-tasking increases stress hormones, causing overstimulation, mental fog and an inability to focus. Sounds right to me as I sit here trying to write! A less obvious consequence is that going for our phones robs us of the creativity that is born in boredom.

Crazy Busy by Kevin DeYoung discusses our culture of distraction to the point of addiction and the effects it has both on us and on our kids.[58] He goes on to discuss the distracting effect of technology in our lives today. I'm afraid I might have to agree with DeYoung when he says, 'I can't seem to work for more than fifteen minutes without getting the urge to check my email, glance at a blog, or get caught up on Twitter. It's a terrible feeling.' Writing this book has me constantly searching for ways to distract myself from the difficulty of the task!

He quotes Richard John Neuhaus, who explains the effect of technology as an old word, 'acedia':

> *Acedia is evenings without number obliterated by television, evenings neither of entertainment nor of education but of narcoticized defence against time and duty. Above all, acedia is apathy, the refusal to engage the pathos of other lives and of God's life with them.*[59]

This, to me, is the crux of our cultural problem. We're content to let our stresses be soothed away by the distractions created by others. We live with the false belief that this is somehow productive or useful. My son said once, in an effort to take back control (he gets mesmerised into a state of paralysis!), that he wanted to 'create more than he consumed'. I think it's a worthy goal for all of us to balance the effect of technology.

Technology disconnects us from people. We are social creatures, and before we know it, we become lonely or lulled into a mild state of depression, which we soothe away with another dose of technology, and this dulls us to the needs and joys of a life of meaning and purpose.

Recently, science reporter Brian Resnick reviewed the effect of smartphones on a whole generation.[60] He began with very troubling statistics about the increase in teen suicide. He refers to generational psychology researcher Jean Twenge who in 2017 made frightening connections between technology use and mental health issues in teenagers.[61] She found that anxiety and depression had leapt upwards in teenage girls in 2012 when iPhones became commonplace. Every parent's nightmare.

Resnick's article is a useful exercise in balance if not in answers. He reports:

> *Important nuance is missing if we just talk about digital technologies in general, Amy Orben, a psychologist also with the Oxford Internet Institute, says. 'Scrolling through skinny Instagram models will naturally have very different effects than Skyping your grandmother or chatting with your school classmates. … I analyzed all possible paths [through the data]', Orben says, 'and I found that you could have written hundreds of thousands of papers that showed a negative correlation between digital technologies and well-being; another couple thousand with non-significant effects, which probably wouldn't even have been published; and then some with positive. And there, we already see what a mess this is.'*

Another useful and nuanced report researched whether social media posed a threat to young people's well-being. Written by the Happiness Research Institute in 2019, this report explored which variables made a difference.[62] Girls seemed to be more dependent than boys, but this only posed a problem if they also felt emotionally unsupported by their parents. Using social media for active communication had positive outcomes, but when used for passive consumption of others' content, young people felt more lonely and ashamed. They found a connection between unhappiness and frequency of use but were unable to determine which direction was causal.

I actually find it helpful to consider things a complex mess. We often try to over-simplify things. This makes outrage, avoidance and side-stepping issues possible. I really like this comment from Resnick that sums up his article:

After all, there are endless variables that can come to influence kids' well-being – their parents, their socioeconomic status, their exposure to environmental toxins, whether they're read to as kids, and so on. What if it's the case that in that mix, digital technology use barely nudges the needle? There might be more powerful interventions – like helping to eliminate childhood poverty – that are more worthy of concern and policy focus.[63]

In Chapter 9 we'll turn our attention to the worthy concern of children in poverty. Technology and our children are definitely concerning though, so we'll need some good conversations to work our way through it. Be sure to look at the technology conversations in Chapter 6.

Parents' work leading to stress

In *Crazy Busy*, Kevin DeYoung investigates the effect we have on our children as parents and concludes that it's not quite as spectacular as we'd like to think:

> *We think of our children as amazingly fragile and entirely moldable. Both assumptions are mistaken. It's harder to ruin our kids than we think and harder to stamp them for success than we'd like.... Kids are safer than ever before, but parental anxiety is skyrocketing. Children have more options and more opportunities, but parents have more worry and hassle.*[64]

He writes about a survey called 'Ask the Children' by researcher Ellen Galinsky. She interviewed more than a thousand children in primary school. She asked the kids what one thing they would change about the way their parents' work was affecting them. **They answered that they wished their parents were less tired and less stressed.** The kids knew their parents loved them, but their parent's biggest weakness, they thought, was anger management. More than 40 percent of kids gave their parents a worse grade on controlling their temper than anything else! Stress will do that to anyone.

Crazy Busy argues for a simplification of our lives, and Kevin suggests that we might have made parenting too complex. Seems our character might be more important than our rules or our treats.

Summary

So in today's culture, we have a society full of stressed-out, depressed people who are consuming too much, spending too much time on technology, overcomplicating parenting and working too much.

2. What can we imagine would be better?

The Happiness Trap, by Dr. Russ Harris, suggests values are an antidote to depression.[65] Harris says clients ask him 'What's the point in life?' and 'Why don't I feel excited about anything?' These are universal questions even when we are not depressed, especially for teenagers trying to find their way in the world.

Understanding our values gives clarity about our passions in life: what gives us meaning and purpose to get out of bed in the morning. Our values are our deepest desires – what we believe in, who we want to be. They are guiding principles for relating to the world around us. So one of our conversations will look at our family values too.

Instead of being depressed, stressed-out people who are slaves to our individual-centric, consumerism culture, we can come together to create change. And we can help our own kids create change. I read a great quote once that says, 'As parents, it's not our job to toughen up our children to face a cruel and heartless world. It's our job to raise children who will make the world a little less cruel and heartless.' If we can help to connect children to their own compassion and generosity when they're young, then we'll set the pattern for when they're older.

There's good news everywhere, though. People all over the world are helping each other during the global pandemic crisis. Young people in India delivered aid packages to poor daily workers. Chinese volunteers drove medical staff to work when buses were suspended. South African communities made survival packs, and students in Prague babysat kids for doctors and nurses. Others helped the elderly by organising virtual coffee and counselling groups.[66]

People came together because it was a time of crisis. But what about before a crisis? My brother only met his neighbours when a fire ravaged the suburbs around them, and they were all forced to stand in the street anxiously awaiting their fate. While they waited days for the electricity to come back on, the neighbours ate together on communal barbeques in their cul-de-sac. They've remained friendly ever since, but it took a crisis.

In his book *Sapiens*, Yuval Noah Harari says we have lasted as a species because we are good at cooperating and collaborating.[67]

Now we need to collaborate on many issues to improve our culture, including our economic state. Kate Raworth, an economist who envisaged a new model to replace our current growth-crazy economics systems, says constant growth is no longer feasible on a finite planet. She calls for 'Donut Economics', which helps us find a place for everyone to thrive.[68] It's all about balancing the gap between some having too much and some having too little.

Personally, I like the word 'enough'. Enough conjures sufficiency and contentment, but it also suggests protest: Stop – that's enough! For everyone on the planet to have enough, those of us who are consuming too much will have to find a way to stop the spiralling need for more. Imagine a world where everyone has access to everything they need to flourish. Most recent wars have been fought because of scarcity – desperate, poverty-induced rebellion. Imagine if we eradicated extreme poverty! Imagine if politicians and corporations were less greedy and didn't engage in bullying behaviour. Imagine if our children grew up to be generous and inclusive instead.

Real community will help us imagine how things could be different. There are cultures around the world that have less material wealth but more relational wealth than current Western culture. Imagine a village where children play together, people work and cook and talk together. This is how humanity has lived for ages. High walls and nuclear families have lost this to a great extent. Many families don't even eat or watch television together anymore. Imagine a community with a purpose that gathered everyone together and inspired them to solve problems and create collaboratively. I know such communities exist. I've been part of them, and I've learnt from them.

Our wealth inspired consumerism which inspired technology, and they all started as great things. They're still great things! But everything needs balance. We've let the balance go awry, and it's causing us problems. Imagine if we could wake from this distracted blur and remember what we truly care about. Maybe we'd be less anxious and stressed, and we'd find creative ways to have a healthy work–life balance. Imagine if we learnt from this in time to save our kids! That's my real prayer for this book.

The conversations presented here aim to get us talking together as a family about our responses to wealth, consumerism and technology – for good and bad. And to make plans together for dealing with it. We'll realign our values so we know what our balance should be, and we'll help our kids know the path to true happiness. **And when children's participation is valued and their creativity is accessed, we will all do better.**

In summary, our world could be better if our culture had more balance, more creativity and more sense of community. We have already seen how great change can be made when people come together. If we want to change our culture, we need to work together.

3. What can we change to get there?

Consumerism

One of my favourite events of the year is a 'clothes swap' that our local church puts on. We each bring several items that we no longer wear but are in good condition. We wait with vino and nibbles while the hall is set up like a shop and curtains make a changing room. As we wait, we can survey the 'silent auction' items. Different people have offered their services – gardening, tutoring, art workshops or bird walks, even a holiday home. We write down our bids. A presentation tells us about the 'Ethical Fashion Guide' - we're raising funds to support their research and advocacy to fashion brands. Then we get to try on the clothes. Friends run up to me with items – 'This looks like you!' Then later, 'Oh that's my dress – how wonderful!' It's my favourite way to shop. It ticks so many boxes – a fun evening with friends, new clothes and an advocacy action to tell fashion brands their consumers care about the workers making their clothes.

It's becoming much easier to shop ethically and consume simply.

Apps, magazines and websites exist to help guide us.[69]

- We can invest our money in ways that don't harm the planet.
- We can buy fair-trade chocolate that doesn't rely on modern slavery for our luxury.
- And new industries exist to help us declutter our homes or even move into tiny houses.

Young adults are searching for ways to live simply and sustainably, and they're inspiring their parents.

Along with consuming more ethically, we need to change how much we consume. These changes don't need to start on a global scale. There is another way. We can give families opportunities to intentionally work together to build contentment, generosity and compassion. If we want our children to grow up content and to know when enough is enough, we can begin by educating them about the agenda of the advertising industry and helping them to understand the effects of retail therapy. Knowledge is the beginning of the power to disregard them. In a very mobile and multi-cultural society, families are looking for support in the absence of extended family and in the face of competing voices. This book aims to take a step towards providing it!

One way to help our kids consume less is to do as researcher Paul Piff suggests. He found that watching a short video on child poverty was enough to increase our willingness to help a stranger.[70] Small changes in our values and perspectives can restore our empathy. This means as parents, we can give our kids information and experiences that will nudge them towards compassion and away from consumerism.

Technology

The technology conversations presented in the next chapter aim to get us talking together as a family about our responses to technology. Whether for good or bad, we can make plans together for dealing with them.

Far from disparaging devices, Dr Kristy Goodwin encourages us to talk with our children about the best ways to use them. Research shows we need to be having age-appropriate conversations with our kids from about six years old.[71] The issue is with us, though, from the earliest moment our kids start watching screens. Every family is different and always changing, so continual conversations about what boundaries work best are necessary – for both children AND parents! Some parents limit screen times to Friday afternoon and weekends. Many use parent control software and have tech-free zones in the house – bedrooms, the dining table, play areas. Parents are often digitally disconnected too – so making family rules that keep everyone accountable is a great idea.

When we visited my father's home as kids, we were shocked at first by the boredom of no television! I've spoken to many kids since who agreed that after the initial shock of this passes, we actually liked the freedom this gave. We discovered made-up games and got creative. This should encourage us that our kids won't starve without devices, but if we can persevere, they might like it too!

Dr Goodwin counselled against digital amputation or complete censorship as punishment, though. Studies show that punishment, while making parents feel better, doesn't work as a teaching method in the long-term. Immediate, intermittent but specific positive reinforcement is much better. Punishing by removing screens is problematic because it decreases the likelihood that our kids will come to us if they find something inappropriate. They'll worry that the device will be removed altogether. So instead, Goodwin suggests designated screen time. Then get the kids outside in nature or doing something physical to calm down their hyper-aroused states. Boys are particularly vulnerable to the sophisticated way games are made to be addictive. Helping them understand this can give them the power to control it themselves.

Technology is here to stay, so increasing our knowledge and control is crucial for all of us. I don't know about you, but buzzing notifications on my phone sure get me jumping, so turning them off is much more relaxing!

A really great technique is to spend time occasionally watching their shows with our kids, or letting them teach us about their games. This increases our opportunities for incidental and teachable conversations. We can even scroll through their social feeds with them, talking about people's hopes for their posts. A conversation that gets them thinking and empowers their own choices will work much better than censorship.

They say knowledge is power, and this is the case in being intentional about the effect our culture is having on us and our children. We can learn from research what best brings about change, and we can practise the skills and tools that make it happen. Some of those things are curiosity, creativity and contentment.

Values

To combat our consumerism and addiction to technology, I imagine we'll need to readjust our values and our sense of community.

We'll need to value fairness and equity for people who are culturally different from us.

We'll need to value something other than our own distraction and entertainment. Imagine if our dependence on consumerism and technology due to boredom or loneliness or stress relief was replaced with passion and purpose. When we're watching television (or devices), we're lulled and we escape, but we don't get up from the couch with our woes fixed and energy fired up. People who have a passion get energised. They're attractive to be around and their enthusiasm is catching. They become creative and inclusive. I'm thinking of someone who cares passionately about the fate of animals or children, someone who rises from the ashes of a tragedy to fight against whatever caused it.

Curiosity and creativity

We're used to people telling us what they're against, but sometimes it's better to spend time thinking about what we're FOR. We can do this by taking time out from the influence our culture has on us through consumerism and technology to let our brains have a play on their own. Kids have a lot to teach us in this!

An active, seeking curiosity is a marvellous thing. People who are generally curious are happier, have more meaning in life and seek out ways to improve themselves. These traits might lead to their better psychological health too. Even more, **curious people cope better with uncertainty and the anxiety it can produce**. They're more likely to respond with playfulness and less likely to be aggressive. It affects attitude too – curious people are less defensive and critical.[72]

I remember going to a counsellor once and telling her that even whilst I was feeling unhappy about whatever it was at the time, I was also interested in my response and that of those around me. She said this was one of the main aims of counselling: to help us get to the point where we could be curious onlookers to our situation to some extent. This one-step-removed viewpoint helps calm any situation. Our aim is not to just react but to be curious about reactions.

This, in turn, positively affects people around us. When we show we're curious about people and interested in them, by asking genuine questions, then those other people find us more engaging to be around. Taking the spotlight off ourselves helps us enjoy experiences more.

And curiosity helps us grow. Dr Todd Kashdan, who wrote the book *Curious* and directs a well-being lab, explains that process like this:

> There is a simple storyline for how curiosity is the engine of growth. By being curious we explore. By exploring, we discover. When this is satisfying we are more likely to repeat it. By repeating it, we develop competence and mastery. By

developing competence and mastery, our knowledge and skills grow. As our knowledge and skills grow, we stretch and expand who we are and what our life is about. By dealing with novelty, we become more experienced and intelligent, and infuse our lives with meaning. Curiosity begets more curiosity because the more we know, the more details there are to attend to, the more we realise what there is to learn.[73]

Curiosity is also a foundational ingredient for creativity. In our world, rote learning knowledge is gone because we can find out anything with a flick of Google. It's the skill to connect knowledge that top executives are after. And that the world needs. That's where creativity comes in. Children are fantastic at divergent thinking – thinking outside the box. Two- to five-year-olds score top marks on divergent thinking tasks. One of the most-watched TED talks is 'Do Schools Kill Creativity?' by Sir Ken Robinson.[74] He talks about education systems needing to adapt to inspire creativity.

The conversations in this book seek to inspire curiosity and creativity in all of your family members. You may find your kids become your teachers in these areas!

Summary

To incite change, we need to learn and implement ways to consume less and more ethically, establish a healthy relationship with technology and increase our curiosity and creativity. A great place to start is with defining and adjusting our values.

Children learn best when they follow their own curiosity, rather than having learning imposed on them.

- Dr A Solter.

My favourite way to learn is by my mistakes.

- Naomi (10).

The more that you read, the more things you will know The more that you learn, the more places you'll go."

- Dr Seuss

CHAPTER 6

CONVERSATIONS ABOUT OUR CULTURE

Review the pre-activity notes for children at the end of the introduction before you begin the conversations. Grab notebooks and choose someone to read.

Building Community

 ## 1. Where we're headed

To see how hospitality lets us combine all our relationship skills so we can build a culture of community.

 ## 2. Packing our bags: what we need to know, or something to stimulate our thinking

My mother's household was very calm and structured – always tidy, carefully decorated, with beautifully tended plants. But no one ever came to visit. This suited me as I was in charge of cooking every night, but it didn't teach me to be generous or community-minded. As kids, we always went out to our friends' houses rather than inviting them over.

My husband's family has a Chinese background, and their life revolved around food! They always had enough for friends who turned up. When I got married, I had to learn to adjust my cooking ratios to allow for unexpected guests! It was a new culture for me to learn.

My decision to become a hospitable person really came after a family trip to another culture in Indonesia. We were part of a big group visiting a series of micro-finance loan projects that we'd raised money to support. The people were very poor, but they cooked for us everywhere we went. Amazing food! I felt humbled and inspired and have been cooking for people to show I care ever since!

Because of this, our children grew up in a home where visitors were always welcome. I loved meeting all of my sons' friends. I asked my son about this just now, and he said he really valued meeting a huge range of people over a meal.

Just as it touched my family, it can touch yours as well. **Engaging in hospitality builds a relational culture because it helps us share our lives with each other**. It's an important symbol of connection and trust and helps us get to know others, which makes it easier to love them. Letting people inside our homes and feeding them is like a gift – it covers a lot of love languages. It also sets the scene for deeper conversations.

3. Reading the map: instructions or preparation

Think about the various houses you've visited and eaten in. How did they differ from your home? How welcome did you feel and why?

4. On the road: our conversation

* How do your friends' homes differ in culture to yours?
* Do you have family mealtimes? Do they stimulate conversations?
* Is cooking something you like or hate doing?
* What other ways could you show hospitality to people?
* What cultures of hospitality have you been exposed to?
* Do you feel any closer to someone once you've eaten with them in their home?
* Does it matter if a home is messy or rich or if the food is perfect or simple to meet the goals of hospitality?

5. Unpacking

* Is this something you value as a family?
* What could you do to make visitors feel more welcome in your home? (e.g., my husband gets them to help with something straight up, so they feel part of things! Win-win!)
* What ways could your family work together to be more welcoming? Who will organise food and who will wash up?

A famous proverb says we should always show hospitality to strangers because you never know when it will be an angel come to visit ☺

 ## 6. Making the journey matter

Invite someone over for a meal. Play a game with them to break the ice. Perhaps ask them if they like cheese?! How would your family like to be more hospitable?

Our Family Values

 1. Where we're headed

We'll create a list of the values our family cherishes so we'll know what to put most of our time, energy and money towards. Sharing these values helps us feel we belong and gives us a way to live purposefully. Knowing deep down what we think is good or bad also helps us make wise choices.

 2. Packing our bags: what we need to know, or something to stimulate our thinking

Try this quick quiz:

1. name the three richest people in the world
2. name the last three Miss Universe winners
3. name three people who have won a Nobel Prize
4. name the last three Oscar-winning directors
5. name the three fastest runners in the world

Can't?

Try this quiz instead ...

1. name three teachers who helped you at school
2. name three friends who have helped you
3. name three people who have taught you something useful
4. name three people who made you feel special
5. name three people whose stories have inspired you

It's not speed or money or beauty or talent that makes a difference in your life. It's the people who cared.

3. Reading the map:
instructions or preparation

Whether we realise it or not, we are deciding on the type of person we will be by what we spend time and effort on. So you might as well be intentional about it! You can tell what you REALLY value by how much time or energy or money you put into something.

Schools usually choose values and so do some organisations. For example, their value might be 'What we receive, we pass on'. Can you share yours?

4. On the road:
our conversation

When we value something, we think our hard work is worth the effort.

How likely are you to put more effort into the things listed below? Place stars next to these words to indicate their importance to you (more stars = more important to you).

* family
* friends
* health
* wealth
* learning
* future career
* faith
* art or music
* adventure
* leisure
* sport
* pets
* environment
* honesty, kindness, generosity
* changing the world!

We need a balance of all these things usually. But unless we decide which ones are most important to us, things get decided for us by other people and circumstances.

5. Unpacking

* What's important to your family?
* Do you value cooking or camping for example?
* Honesty or humility? Forgiveness?
* (You obviously value conversations!)
* What makes you different from other families?
* Finish this sentence – 'In our family we ...'
* Now can you come up with a set of family values together?

 6. Making the journey matter

You could make a poster with words or photos showing things your family values or finds meaningful in life. Remember these are the things we will choose to put more of our time, money and energy towards! Pop your poster on the fridge for a while.

Happiness Check

1. Where we're headed

We're aiming to understand a bit more about getting the right balance for happiness instead of just accepting our culture's definitions of happiness as wealth and fame and stuff. And research shows our home is more important for happiness than income or work, so let's start there![75]

2. Packing our bags: what we need to know, or something to stimulate our thinking

There are three similar-sized parts to happiness.

1. We are born with different degrees of general happiness in our personality.
2. Good and bad things happen to us that affect our happiness temporarily.
3. We can choose our attitude to these things.

The third one is the only one we have much control over, so it makes sense to make the best of this one!

Remember Winnie-the-Pooh? Think about Tigger and Eeyore. Tigger is enthusiastic and full of fun and excited about life. Eeyore is sad and droopy and is always looking at the worst in every situation. He sees the same world as Tigger completely differently! Which one of these characters is more like you? Which one would you like to be like? Our attitude doesn't exactly change the world, but it sure changes the way we experience it! And maybe those near to us too.

Did you know? People around the world were asked how satisfied they were with their life. The four hundred richest people in America scored exactly the same as the Inuit people in Greenland and the

Masai of Kenya, even though the Kenyans had no electricity or running water![76]

According to The Happiness Institute, one of the biggest mistakes people make is looking for happiness in things.[77] Money and possessions are OK, but they only make us happy for a short while. We can <u>choose</u> to be happy, though. Some of the ways we can do this are:

* Having good relationships
* Thinking optimistically
* Having compassion for other people
* Knowing and using our own strengths
* Being grateful

 ## 3. Reading the map: instructions or preparation

Answer these questions in your notebook before you chat together.

How happy are you right now? (Put a cross on the scale)

I feel:

miserable........................good

tired a lot........................energetic and enthusiastic

pessimistic........................optimistic

I have no strengths........................I know and use my strengths

My life is:

boring........................fascinating

no direction or purpose........................my goals are clear

no close friends........................very connected to people

Do you think your happiness is affected by how you see your life?

A happy memory I have is:

When I'm unhappy, it helps if:

I'm grateful for:

4. On the road:
our conversation

* Let each person share some of their thoughts about happiness.
* Can you come up with an example of optimistic thinking (rather than pessimistic)?
* Talk about how you could help each other when you're not feeling happy.
* Focus on one person at a time. Let everyone else suggest a strength they have and could use to create more happiness. Remember to use your listening skills!

5. Unpacking

Decide as a family how you can practise being grateful. Perhaps you could each think of something over dinner or before you go to sleep. Perhaps you could start a 'Gratitude Jar'? Put a notepad and pen beside a big empty jar somewhere easy to find in your house. Every time something good happens, make a note and pop it in the jar. On special occasions, you could pull some out and read them.

6. Making the journey matter

Lots of research has been done into happiness recently. When so many people are suffering from anxiety and depression, it's good for us to understand what things help – for us, and to care for our friends and family.

You can download free resources at https://www.drhappy.com.au/resources/ that explain more about how to be happy![78]

Practising Gratitude

 ## 1. Where we're headed

The most powerful way to combat the effects of consumerism is to practise gratitude. It's also one of the best ways known to increase our happiness – because it increases our contentment.

 ## 2. Packing our bags: what we need to know, or something to stimulate our thinking

Advertising exists to make us think we don't have enough. We're consumed by consumerism when we're tricked into being discontented. Through these feelings of discontent, we lose perspective about what we need versus what we want. The antidote then is to realise this and be grateful for what we do have. Research shows gratitude makes us more content.

The Science of Gratitude lists many benefits of gratitude.[79] They include happiness, life satisfaction, health, resilience, patience, humility and wisdom. Worth doing, huh?!

The best exercise for practising gratitude is called 'Three Good Things'.[80] In an experiment, people were asked to write three good things in their journal every night for a week. They also had to say why they were good. The researchers found that people were happier after one week of doing this! And they kept on getting happier because people enjoyed doing it so kept going!

3. Reading the map:
instructions or preparation

Gratitude is even more effective if you get your feelings involved. That's why we need the 'why' part of the exercise. Do you remember how you felt when someone was kind? How much your grandmother loved you? A wonderful experience? What means so much to you about someone? Thinking about <u>why</u> and feeling it helps get the gratitude to go deeper!

4. On the road:
our conversation

Ease into your gratitude practice with these lists:

* List all the fun things you could do with just one chair
* List things that make you happy (but cost nothing!)
* List the three possessions you'd take if you had to leave home in a hurry

Now try the three good things exercise. Can you keep it up for a week?

5. Unpacking

Share your lists.

* How much overlap is there on your lists of happiness and possessions?
* Will you commit to each do the three good things exercise for a week?

6. Making the journey matter

Check in on each other's happiness levels after a week of remembering 'three good things' each day.

Another experiment had people write and deliver a gratitude letter to someone who had been kind to them. Someone who had never been well thanked. This is a pretty powerful idea ... maybe you'd like to give it a try?

How Much Money Matters?

 ## 1. Where we're headed

Everyone knows not having enough money is a problem, but sometimes having too much is too! This discussion is to help us work out how much money is enough and to make sure we use money in line with our values.

 ## 2. Packing our bags: what we need to know, or something to stimulate our thinking

Did you know we learn our money habits well before our tenth birthday?[81] Money can create strong emotional reactions in us. People can be greedy, arrogant, jealous and even hurt others for money. Because we don't find it polite to talk in detail about money in our society, we grow up not understanding it very well.

How can money help us with our values, goals and well-being? Can it make us happier?

Advertising won't help us here – spending more money is their goal. Our communities might not help either – people around us might have different values and our human need to be accepted confuses us into wanting to be like others.

Even our family conversations might not include money, especially if grandparents didn't talk about or handle money well either. Research shows parents are more comfortable talking about sex with their children than money![82]

I heard of one family who brought home their weekly pay as coins. A LOT of coins! They dumped them on the dining room table and the kids thought they were rich! Then they started dividing it into piles to pay the bills ...

3. Reading the map: instructions or preparation

In the last couple of generations, people's wealth has increased a lot. Homes are bigger and holidays fancier than when I was young. Debt has increased too, though. Research shows that the relationship between money and happiness is complex.[83]

If people don't have enough money to live, more money makes them happy.

If people have more money but spend it on materialistic goals, it makes them unhappy.

If people have more money and use it according to values to meet their personal goals, it makes them happier.

Make sure everyone understands the definitions of words as you're discussing the following questions. The idea is just to start a conversation.

4. On the road: our conversation

* Do your values help you decide how much money you need?
* How do your values affect the way you spend money?
* Do you value being careful with money and not wasteful?
* Are you happy to wait until you've saved before you buy?
* So, do you value saving?
* Is buying on credit OK?
* Is insurance important? Why?
* How do you feel about owing people money?
* How important is generosity?
* Do you have a budget?
* Does money cause you happiness or stress?
* Do you feel like a slave to money or is it a practical help?

5. Unpacking

* Did you have any disagreements in your family?
* Did your discussion get emotional?
* Was it worthwhile?
* Write down anything specific that you've decided to change, do or follow up on as a result.

 ## 6. Making the journey matter

If your family enjoyed this discussion, *The Barefoot Investor for Families* by Scott Pape is extremely popular in Australia and fun to read.

Consumed or Contented?

 ## 1. Where we're headed

To find contentment by gaining a bit of global perspective.

 ## 2. Packing our bags: what we need to know, or something to stimulate our thinking

If everyone around us has the same amount of stuff as us (a house, a car, toys, whatever), we're pretty content. But what if everyone around us has much more than we do? Imagine hungry village children seeing a TV in a shopfront playing an American sitcom! Suddenly, they are less content! They feel 'relatively deprived'.

Consumerism is the strong desire to get more stuff. It's led by the advertising industry. Consumerism makes us feel relatively deprived so we think we deserve more toys or clothes or things. It turns wants into needs. This discussion aims to raise our awareness of this difference by making our reference point more global.

'Dollar Street' was set up by a not-for-profit educational organisation that wants to help us become more aware of this. The website shows photographs of different families around the world. You can search by income or by country, and choose to compare everything from beds to bikes, from toys to toilets! This is a great tool for broadening our perspective.

3. Reading the map:
instructions or preparation

On a scale from 1–5, where one is extremely poor and five is extremely rich, where do you think your family sits?

* On a big screen, visit https://www.gapminder.org/dollar-street/ matrix.
* Click on 'Families' and choose what you'd like to compare.
* Click on 'the World' to choose countries.
* Choose income levels by moving the slider from 'poorest' to 'richest'.

4. On the road:
our conversation

* What did you find interesting about your exploration on Dollar Street?
* When you have spare time, what do you like to do?
* Do you need to buy something to do this?
* What do you need to have a good life?
* What makes you happier for longer? New things or playing with friends and family?
* How much do you like to share?
* How much do you think advertising affects you?

Now visit www.footprintcalculator.org and take their quiz.

It works out how many planets' worth of resources your family is consuming. Imagine if everyone in the world lived like you.

What difference does this make to you as a family?

5. Unpacking

Remember your number from the start? On a scale from 1–5, where one is extremely poor and five is extremely rich, where do you think your family sits? Would you like to change your number now?

What are some things you are grateful for? What could you give up or do less of?

6. Making the journey matter

Play a game of 'Rigged Monopoly' to notice the effect wealth has on us. Roll the dice before you start to choose one 'special' person. They will start the game with twice as much money as all the other players. This person will also get twice as much money each time they pass GO. Give this person extra snacks. Play the game, then discuss everyone's feelings about the outcome!

Visit https://fashionfootprint.org/ (then learn to sew a button back on!)

Visit www.storyofstuff.org for more ideas – they're cool.

Finding Contentment
Without Stuff

 ## 1. Where we're headed

Thinking about the difference between needs and wants to cut down on consumerism.

 ## 2. Packing our bags: what we need to know, or something to stimulate our thinking

When I finished university, I worked to save up and then went travelling in Europe. It was amazing, and I felt brave and sometimes lonely, but I learnt that I can look after myself. For nearly a year, I carried everything I needed in a backpack. Because I hate carrying heavy things, I never had too much! One of the best things I learnt was that I really don't need much. It felt freeing to realise how little stuff I really needed. And how content I was without it.

It's easy to get caught in the trap of thinking that having more 'things' will make you happy. Wouldn't it be great if we could want more of what really matters instead?

 ## 3. Reading the map: instructions or preparation

Think of a really long time. The longest you can. Your whole life even.

What really matters most? What things should we devote our lives to?

You're going to need some props for this trip. Collect two different coloured stickers or Post-it notes – enough for you all to have about 10 each. Then find an empty box or bag or two for each person.

4. On the road: our conversation

Walk around your home together and put one coloured sticker or note on the things you couldn't live without. Put another colour on the things you really like.

Carry an empty box with you for the things you realise you don't really need or want.

(Maybe two boxes – one for things that someone else might want that you could give away).

5. Unpacking

Walk around the house and look at what everyone else put sticky notes on. Did anything stand out or surprise you? Talk about this exercise together.

Was it hard? Or surprisingly easy?
* How do you feel about the amount of stuff you have?
* Can you imagine wanting less would be helpful?

6. Making the journey matter

Could you actually give away some of the things you collected? There are lots of books and apps around now to help you declutter your home in order to declutter your mind. Pick a room to become more content in today!

The happiest people don't have the best of everything – they just make the best of everything they have.

Creating Creativity

 ## 1. Where we're headed

One way to make sure we're not consumed by consumerism is to create more than we consume! Creativity is very good for us, but we can lose it or be distracted from it. Since children are great at creativity, they can help their parents become more creative.

 ## 2. Packing our bags: what we need to know, or something to stimulate our thinking

Most top executives say that creativity is more important than intelligence. The internet means that so much knowledge is available to us, but it's working out what to do with it that's useful. Did you know that kids can think much more creatively than adults? Most (98 percent) two- to five-year-olds score as geniuses on creative thinking![84]

Kids have it and businesses want it. So: we can learn from kids! It's a skill that declines with age – possibly because we stop using it!

Children have better memories than adults too. They learn much faster and think more broadly.

My son decided to try to create more than he consumes. He wrote poems or played drums instead of watching so much YouTube. Whenever you make something new, you are creating. Writing a story, painting a picture, or solving a problem are all creative. Seeing the world from different perspectives is creative – so sharing your different perspectives with each other is helpful.

Creativity allows us to

* come up with new inventions
* imagine future possibilities
* explore new ways of thinking and acting
* cope when things change

* solve problems
* get more out of life.[85]

As the great artist Pablo Picasso said, 'Every child is an artist. The problem is how to remain an artist when they grow up.'

3. Reading the map: instructions or preparation

You can encourage your own creativity by practising it, just like any skill or talent. The brain is like a muscle that gets stronger the more you use it. When you learn, neurons in the brain grow new connections. This means that you can take charge of how smart you want to be! As one boy realised, 'You mean I don't have to be dumb?'

Creativity researchers agree that you'll need to persevere and have a 'growth mindset'. A growth mindset means you know you can get better at something by trying harder or practising more – that you're not limited (with a 'fixed mindset'). Research shows our brains are amazing at growing and learning new things, which is important for all of life! So keep trying and believe that you can get better at it![86]

Pick one or many of these ideas to enhance your creativity. All you need is a bit of time, so switch off your devices and try these … I wonder what you will create?!

4. On the road: our conversation

* Tell a joke. Creativity works best when you can laugh.
* Write down everything you think is interesting about a butterfly, a peanut and singing.
* Try finger painting or make playdough to get in touch with your inner child!
* Write a list of what's fantastic about your life right now.
* What fantastic things can you imagine in your future?
* Give everyone ten pieces of Lego and see what they can create.
* Draw a floor plan of your dream house. Put in anything you like – the odder the better.

- Make up a story that connects these random words: drop, elephant, shower, moon, earring, fabulous.
- Write a list of things you want to change.
- Share or think up your own favourite ways to create!

5. Unpacking

- Talk together about how it felt to enter a creative zone.
- Were you disappointed with your current creative skill level?
- Are you inspired to try something else?

6. Making the journey matter

Use your notebook as a journal for creative ideas. Write down interesting things you notice or feel.

Take a cold shower – running water increases creativity and cold jumpstarts your brain!

Nature inspires creativity too – go for a walk! Make a movie of the walk and edit it. Study a book of jokes to work out what makes them funny, and then try to make up your own.

There's a great little article you can read together. It's about how creativity is used for music, for jokes, for curing diseases and for building businesses. Find it at https://mintzberg.org/blog/creativity and read it for inspiration for your next creativity time.[87]

Taming Technology

 ## 1. Where we're headed

To come to some family agreement about the merits of technology and decide what will work best for your family.

 ## 2. Packing our bags: what we need to know, or something to stimulate our thinking

In Zimbabwe, the Information Communication Technology minister stated that *'broadband connectivity is no longer a luxury but a right.'*[88] Do you think the internet is a modern human right, like food and water?

Around the world, people are getting vital information about COVID-19 and other dangers from the internet. News services, social media posts and group messaging connect us. And despite the lockdown, people can continue to work online.

At the same time, research shows our excessive use of smartphones and social media is making us less able to focus, and possibly more depressed and anxious. There's still debate though. It could be complicated. Perhaps the highest users of tech have problems, but the average teenager doesn't? Or do you think the average teenager does have problems? Online gaming is huge. Families argue over how much time is enough and many are feeling less 'connected' IRL (or for parents: in real life).

3. Reading the map: instructions or preparation

* Make a list of all the things you use the internet for.
* Estimate how much time you personally spend connected to tech devices.
* Is your use of social media more active (posting and directly communicating with friends) or passive (just consuming content)?
* Do you use social media more when you are happy or unhappy? How do you feel after a scrolling session?

4. On the road: our conversation

Imagine there is an invisible line from one end of the room to the other.

One end is 'I agree' and the other end is 'I disagree'.

Kids: Stand up and line up along the line according to how much you agree with this statement: my parents spend too much time on screens at home.

Parents: Stand up and line up along the agree-disagree axis: my children spend too much time on screens at home.

Everyone: Try *I spend too much time on screens*, then *I love technology*. Think up more!

Were the results surprising? Did you disagree?

5. Unpacking

* Have a conversation about what you NEED technology for, and what you WANT it for.
* Talk about the effects of social media or games in your family.
* Talk about how much is too much and what limits might work for your family.
* What help might you need to stick to these limits?

6. Making the journey matter

Set up a method for checking on everyone's limits. You could keep a diary for a week, or use technology itself to measure your time on different sites.

You could watch the film 'The Social Dilemma' together to see other families and their ideas.

Tough Tech Talk

 ## 1. Where we're headed

To start a conversation about the darker sides of technology so we can agree on what is not okay and why.

 ## 2. Packing our bags: what we need to know, or something to stimulate our thinking

Sometimes when we hear about the problems with technology, we just roll our eyes and ignore them. Why do you think that is? Because it doesn't apply to us? Are we afraid we might have to stop?

It's not just about the amount of time, but what is being consumed and what is said. When my boys were young, we walked in on them watching pole dancing. I'm not sure who was more shocked, them or us?! Now research shows it's very hard to ignore pornography and it's getting further from real life.

Youth anxiety and depression have been linked to social media and cyberbullying. Suicide is one of the biggest causes of death in young people. These problems alone mean we should talk about them.

 ## 3. Reading the map: instructions or preparation

The key to tricky conversations is to try to keep our emotions out of it as we listen to everyone's point of view calmly. We're more likely to feel comfortable talking about it if we feel heard and understood without judgement. Remember that everyone's number one priority is to care for each other.

We're just going to listen to each other's point of view about some of the issues in a general sense.

4. On the road: our conversation

* What do you think are the main differences between face-to-face communication and texting or posting?
* Is cyberbullying better or worse than real-life bullying?
    * Hint: Do things like audience size, speed of reach, repeat viewing matter?
* Can you be friends with someone online you've never met?
* Can you be friends with your parents online?
* Can you break up with someone online?
* Do manners matter?
* What are some of the problems with more people watching porn?
    * Hint: unrealistic understanding of sex, relationships and what people want IRL (in real life).
* What are some of your fears about young people watching porn?

5. Unpacking

* How do you feel after talking about this tough stuff? Was it embarrassing? Annoying?
* Are you more or less worried than at the start of the conversation?
* Will you do anything differently now?

6. Making the journey matter

What plans can you put in place for talking about your tech fears before they get too big?

Can you design some family guidelines to help each other?

CHAPTER 7

CARING ABOUT OUR INNER SELVES

What do you want people to say about you at your funeral? David Brooks, in his marvellous book *The Road to Character*, helps us think about our aims as people (and as parents).[89] He suggests we think about the difference between writing our CV or resume virtues and writing our eulogy virtues. We list our learning and skills and achievements on our resumes. Thinking about our funeral, though, we have a unique opportunity to consider whether these are the virtues we want people to remember us by. In a eulogy, we hear about whether someone we cared about was kind or brave or honest or faithful. These virtues relate to relationships rather than to success. We see love on show. **At a funeral, we remember, for a moment, what stuff matters.**

Most of the time, though, our education systems, our career-climbing opportunities and our celebrity culture overlook eulogy virtues. But these virtues help decide how close and loving our relationships will be. When my kids thank me for helping them these days, I say, 'That's OK, just take me to the movies when I'm old.' I'm not worried I won't be able to afford it myself – I want them to still love me enough to spend time with me!

While developing our character and our eulogy values are important, Brooks calls for something even greater: **developing our personal character for a social purpose**. Imagine neighbourhoods being places where we can choose to connect and look out for each other, where social change can occur. Rather than trying to save one person at a time (say with a scholarship or via a charity), Brooks suggests we become people who care *together*.

We've probably all noticed the change in social cohesiveness in our local neighbourhoods. When I was growing up, we knew all our neighbours. I've lived on the same street for the last twenty years and watched an incredible turnover as people moved on. Fences feature. One good outcome of the COVID-19 pandemic has been stories of neighbours looking out for one another during lockdowns. As parents, we want values for our kids that will help them have happy, loving lives, but we could think even further.

As a society, we also need kids who think beyond themselves to how they can help *others* have happy, loving lives. These kids would understand that they are part of the 'Common Good'. The philosophy of the Common Good says that we cannot be truly happy if others are suffering. Utilitarianism, by contrast, is another philosophy for making decisions that says we should do what's best for the majority. The Common Good suggests we make decisions based on what's going to be equitably good for everyone. Much harder, but much more satisfying for everyone. This chapter is my attempt to encourage us as families to grow skills and virtues that will lead us closer to the Common Good. The concept of drawing closer to the Common Good brings to mind spirituality.

For me, 'soul' or 'spirit' are big words that encompass not only what is unknown and mystical in the world but also what gives meaning and purpose to our worlds. All humans have sought to describe this in various ways throughout history – it's definitely part of who we are! By tapping into our spiritual side, we can have a better relationship with ourselves and foster a better character. **In this section, we will be paying attention to character and soul as a way to care for our inner selves.**

In my mid-twenties, I lost my sister to a drunk driver. At the time, I was very anti-religion because my dad had grown up in a sect and got kicked out when he questioned their more bizarre practices. But then I met a boy. He danced with me! He was lovely in every way but one – he was a Christian. Serious cognitive dissonance set in, because he seemed so smart and normal - and lovely!

For a year I led this strange life where I went to church with him to seek understanding and to make him keep liking me. I read books and talked to friends to argue my way through all the reasons his beliefs were ridiculous. Yet, the opposite happened: I became astonished by the depth of research and historical data at the foundation of his beliefs. But what moved me most was the spiritual quality of the people. It wasn't only this boy who was lovely.

Love, joy, peace, patience, kindness, goodness, faithfulness, gentleness and self-control. These were the attributes my new Christian friends were seeking in their inner lives. The basic tenet of all major religions is, in fact, the same: treat others the way you would like to be treated. It seems to me the world would be a much better place if everyone tried to live like this!

I've come to see that a healthy inner life, for all of us, is about seeking values like honesty and gratitude and generosity. These habits of character need to be cultivated. Research in the fairly new field of positive psychology is starting to show that if we grow our character, life is better for us. My life has certainly been better since I started cultivating a spiritual inner life. Oh, and I married that lovely boy. :)

1. How are we going now?

In our current Western culture, values are encouraged in schools and souls are discussed in churches (less widespread as not everyone attends church), but our characters get overlooked. This lack of focus on our characters and, for some of us, our souls, has dire consequences. As our social cohesion breaks down with wealth inequality, people trust each other less. As social media takes over our news, we're becoming more divided in our opinions and beliefs. We're beginning to fear or even hate 'the other side'. Knowing every bad thing in the world, together with frustration about the effectiveness of politics, leads to a lack of hope about the future. A breakdown in community leads to less compassion and generosity towards our neighbours. And without purpose or meaning, people seek distraction. In the end, these are all matters of character, of our connection to our own integrity, to our soul.

Hiding our inner selves

I have a little old book published in 1984 that was popular just after I lost my sister and started thinking about the meaning of life. Written by counsellors Lawrence J. Crabb, Jr and Dan B. Allender, *Encouragement – The Key to Caring* talks very practically about how to be a good friend.[90]

The basic premise of *Encouragement* is that we are all walking around with little balls of fear inside us. Even as children, we begin building defensive layers to hide our fear behind. Crabb describes it like this:

> *Whenever we discover a protective strategy that works, we keep it available to put on as a layer whenever we feel the chill of developing rejection. Fear-inspired ingenuity is capable of thinking up an endless variety of protective strategies: jokes, silliness, a cocky attitude, boasting, manipulative tears, feigned repentance and humility, remaining quiet, a drink before meeting friends, spending hours doing homework with our children, or watching television – anything that enables us to greet the world with our real selves hidden safely from sight.[91]*

The problem with this is keeping our inner selves hidden through layers of defence strategies is not good for our souls. Having a strong character means protecting our souls by being true to ourselves and our values, rather than to our defence strategies. It's harder, but better for us in the long run. We need to replace our defence strategies with integrity to feel good about ourselves. **Certainly, we want to raise our children to have a strong enough character to withstand the trials of peer group pressure, let alone the distractions of our culture.**

The other problem is that it affects our relationships. We all run around interacting layer-to-layer, producing surface interactions. We each have a deep fear that our longing to be treated as valuable and significant may never be met. The book goes on to say that we need to find a way to seek a safe source of encouragement for ourselves. Only then can we shed some of our defensive layers and give gifts of encouragement to others so they might be able to shed some layers too. The book's paradigm is within the Christian faith, finding a sense of worth in God. At the time, this, and many other books I read, made sense to me.

Years later, I've seen the reality of this little book's premise in the lives of people I've done life with for decades. Walking with friends through their depression, divorce and death brought it to life. I know how very hard it is to meet people with our defences down, but how incredibly enriching it is when it happens. I think if we can raise kids with a deep understanding of their worth, and encourage them to interact without defensiveness, then they will be free to offer this encouragement to others too. Big call, but this is what it will take.

Lack of soul attention

Church communities can help build character, but many young people are moving further and further away from organised religion. As a young adult, I went trekking in Nepal. It's the most beautiful place – glancing up at the clouds always requires a double-take; they're not clouds up there in the sky, they're mountains! Breathtaking! The towns are a feast for the senses. There are brightly coloured signs and markets. Motorbike noises, spice and animal smells, and delicious food assail your senses. And they have a wild variety of spiritual experiences on offer.

I met a Danish guy in Kathmandu who ran a halfway house for young tourists who had overdosed on spiritual experiences. Trying out Eastern meditation practices without a proper guide sometimes resulted in psychedelic consequences. In the crazy traffic, this could be dangerous! He asked me why these young people who were clearly seeking spiritual things were not finding them in churches at home. At the time I had just come from a small church where the older people attended in suits and ties and ran inquisitions for the youth leaders. I could well imagine why not.

My father grew up in the Exclusive Brethren. They are a sect based on Christianity that tries to live as separately as possible from the world. During his childhood, Dad was unable to play sports, listen to the radio or have friends outside this group. They became wealthy doing business with each other. I say 'sect' because it got weird and antithetical to the rest of orthodox Christianity. When Dad came home from university, he started questioning some of their more extreme practices. Their response was to withdraw from him – he could no longer eat with the family! Then they stopped anyone else from going to university. I grew up unaware of any relatives on Dad's side of the family because they had cast him out. Needless to say, we were, as a family, pretty anti-religion. We knew that Dad was more honest than everyone else, and gentle and kind, but it was a long while before I realised that these character traits were developed by his early faith. Dad is still grateful for his faithful upbringing though.

I relate all this to say: I am well aware of the complexity of the success and failure of those who live with or without attention to soul – and that it's worse when words do not match actions. Heartbreaking even. But these stories are not at all the experience I've had raising my kids within a church community for the last thirty years. It's been my village and it's been life-giving for our family. I'm talking deep connection with integrity, not token words, with real action for love and justice. This disconnect seems to be familiar in our current culture. My faith though, has given me deep connection to meaning and purpose – culminating in this book!

Lack of direction or purpose

Without a clear sense of direction and goals, we are not building soul nor character with purpose. Our inner selves crave meaning as it's an important part of inner peace. Also, a big part of developing a good character is having a strong sense of responsibility and a desire to contribute, but this seems to be lost in our current society. Yuval Noah Harari, who wrote bestseller *Sapiens: A Brief History of Humankind*, concludes his huge book with these thoughts to ponder:

Despite the astonishing things that humans are capable of doing, we remain unsure of our goals and we seem to be as discontented as ever. We have advanced from canoes to galleys to steamships to space shuttles – but nobody knows where we're going. We are more powerful than ever but have very little idea what to do with all that power. Worse still, humans seem to be more irresponsible than ever. ... Is there anything more dangerous than dissatisfied and irresponsible gods who don't know what they want?[92]

Perhaps today so many of us seek distraction as pleasure because we've lost our sense of meaning and purpose.

Are we building a framework for meaning in our families? Are we giving our children a sense of purpose and responsibility for the world around them? Can we help them find the ways they want to contribute to it? I'm hoping the conversations in this section might help.

Summary

Currently, we are engaged in so many distractions that we aren't building our inner selves. Too many of us are hiding behind layers of defence mechanisms, resulting in superficial relationships and a lack of connection to our souls. With lost values and a move away from organised religion, we aren't strengthening our characters and our souls. Essentially, we are wandering around, living without meaning or purpose.

2. What can we imagine would be better?

Meaning and purpose

It's hard to maintain a strong character in the face of distractions without a strong sense of purpose. I found one of my purposes while watching *The Mission*. I don't recommend this movie.[93] It's long and depressing (but with a gorgeous soundtrack by Ennio Morricone that I do recommend). It did, however, change the direction of my life. It stars Jeremy Irons and Robert de Niro as two Catholic priests in 18th century South America. De Niro was a slave trader who had a personal crisis that led him to the priesthood, serving a small community of Indigenous people in the jungle. When politics turn sour, they're told to leave the mission, which will also leave the people without protection from slave traders. The priests agree they will not leave, but clash on the way forward.

De Niro wants to teach these peaceful people to fight to defend themselves. Irons says no: 'If might is right, then love has no place in the world, and I can't live in a world like that.' He leads the women and children in candlelight chorus as the final fight leads to its dreadful conclusion. Morricone's hauntingly beautiful musical score juxtaposes the best and the worst of humankind. The movie is yet another tale of man's inhumanity to man, but movies move us. At that moment I pledged that my life would be on the side of peace, of making things better, not worse, in this world. This purpose still gets me out of bed decades later.

Imagine a world where our children have a deep and positive sense of meaning and purpose in life. Having such a deep purpose will build their character. Sometimes this is referred to as spirituality. Something that helps a person frame and deal with life's randomness and difficulties is worthwhile. Something that reminds us we can be better, that we can contribute and that this will make a difference. I've found this to be very helpful for me, and my sons have benefitted from a spiritual framework for life too.

A fabulous book called *Man's Search for Meaning* by Viktor Frankl speaks powerfully to our need for meaning.[94] While his contemporary, Sigmund Freud, was saying life was all about pleasure, Frankl was in a concentration camp during World War II where people had every avenue for pleasure denied them. His psychological theory of meaning derived from those people that he saw survive and even thrive in the camps. The people who had loved ones to care for or poetry still to write kept their spirits up. They kept hope because they had a reason driving them to go on.

Frankl's further research led him to believe that we all need a project – something we can build or bring into this world.

Investing in younger generations, as a parent, grandparent, teacher or kids or youth leader is a hugely meaningful project! We also need to work at having an optimistic perspective. Hope happens when we remember to look for the good despite the bad. And meaning most often comes within community, whether it's family, friends, work, or play. Imagine a world where everyone had meaning and purpose.

A world full of community and strong connections

As we imagine a better world full of strong integrity, we can see people coming together with a deep sense of community.

Religions help build character because they form a community. A friend told me about a book he'd read called *Who Needs God* by a rabbi, Harold Kushner.[95] Kushner explains that we get the word 'religion' from a Latin word that also gives us the word 'ligament'. They both have the idea of holding something together. I like this. What do you think religion is trying to hold together? Maybe it's the way we make connections between people? Maybe between people and our Higher Power? Something holding together the paradox of good and evil in all of us, of blessing and suffering. Then there's the connection between us and our planet. Asking these big questions is part of being human, and helping our kids wonder about big questions will help them build a framework of meaning for their lives.

Faith gives us meaning and purpose, but also community. It gives us identity and a place to do life with people who are also seeking to live in the world with strong connections. It doesn't make the news, but ask anyone who is part of a faith community how it helps them live.

Summary

A world full of people with strong purposes who unite together in a sense of community is a world that is too strong to break. A world that doesn't fall apart. And to me, this is an (aspirational) essence of the way Jesus suggested we should live together.

3. What can we change to get there?

Understanding the difference between happiness and contentment

When I worked for Tearfund, an aid and development organisation, I went on a trip to Nepal to visit the projects we supported. I was in education, so I was collecting stories to come back and tell people about them. Our guide for part of the trip was Neeraj, a lovely young man who had fabulous English. Whilst he was from a very poor family, a missionary paid for him to study engineering at a university in America. We chatted about many things as we travelled between villages. I was often painfully aware of the difference in financial circumstances between our small group from Australia and the people we were visiting. We each had a large suitcase filled with high-tech, warm clothing, while Neeraj carried one small backpack for his one set of clothes. At one point I asked Neeraj about his take on this, and about greed in general. I think I expected a comment about the almost outrageous wealth of the West needing to filter more into poorer parts of the world. Instead, Neeraj talked about the practical process he and his wife used for making sure they didn't become greedy, which made them happy. All wealth is relative, but the sort of character that works to correct greed in the human heart crosses all boundaries.

We all want our children to be happy, but research is showing us that the way to get there is not what our culture is leading us to believe. Happiness can't be manufactured from stuff; it comes from helping people, from being grateful, from giving generously. What can be created is contentment – it's a choice, an attitude. Helping our kids build characters that value these attitudes will ensure their inner happiness. Did the conversations about consumerism in the last section help your family think more about true happiness? Practising gratitude and generosity and choosing to be content are ways we can help ensure our children's lasting happiness.

Decreased anxiety and depression

In contrast, anxiety and depression are widespread and growing, so any attention to our inner selves needs to be of help here. More than 10 percent of Australians use antidepressants and this has tripled since 2000.[96] I know these medications have helped many people, and I know parents who don't give them to their children lightly, but it's concerning when we think about the cultural implications. Why might this be?

In his inspiring book, *Lost Connections: Why You're Depressed and How to Find Hope*, Johann Hari researches nine different causes for depression and anxiety.[97] Only one of these is biologically based. He discusses our disconnection from various meaningful areas of life: work, a hopeful or secure future, from other people, from the natural world and from meaningful values. Our opportunity to connect to meaningful work decreases with an increasingly casualised labour force. With all the negativity in the world, we have become less hopeful and less secure about the future. The disconnection from work and from hope were already growing before COVID-19 hit. However, it's disconnection from meaningful values that is most pertinent in a chapter about inner selves. Best of all, Hari's wonderful book spends time looking at solutions.

In an effort to value contentment rather than consumerism, Hari reports that in 2007 a city in Brazil banned outdoor advertising with a 'Clean City Law'. Surveys of residents showed they were happier, and somehow psychologically clearer, without the constant call to want more stuff. Some countries have banned advertising directed at children; some have called for devaluing sex and valuing humans; activist groups work against ads that overly sexualise women.

Research into people's values around money found that 'spending often isn't about the object itself. It is about getting to a psychological state that makes you feel better'. When asked what people really value, one young teenage boy answered simply: 'love'. Asking two simple questions about *what people spend on* and *what they value* helped them see the disconnect. Further research showed that buying stuff was only fleetingly helpful and left a gnawing discontent. When researchers asked people to discuss their inner values, they realised how rare these conversations were, because people found this difficult. With all this materialism and lack of articulated values, more and more people struggled with anxiety and depression. The small conversations about values were enough to significantly reduce their levels of materialism and increase their self-esteem!

The research also showed that a community – being surrounded by people to have meaningful and accountable conversations with – was vital to this change. Their community helped people grow their characters and their souls. I'm hoping that the activities that follow will lead to great conversations that grow your family's inner lives.

Character strengths

Thinking about our character is a worthwhile human pursuit. It can help us find the true happiness that comes from meaning and purpose and from interdependent relationships – where we choose to depend on each other. While great religions have been pointing us towards this throughout human history, today this wisdom is supplemented with clear research telling us how to be grateful, how best to be loving and joyous and peaceful and patient and kind. It's not always easy, but it's better than the constant discontent of our current economic system!

Multi-disciplinary professor Dr. Roger Walsh wrote a helpful book called *Essential Spirituality*.[98] He studied the major world religions of Christianity, Islam, Hinduism, Judaism and Buddhism and discovered that they all have some practices in common: They help us look for happiness in the right places and to cultivate love over fear. They encourage our ethics and wisdom in order to serve others.

There's an overlap with positive psychology's research into character strengths too. The VIA Institute on Character[99] has combined research to classify broad categories of common virtues like wisdom and courage, which divide further into traits like curiosity, perseverance, kindness and fairness.

There's also a survey to help people understand and develop their character and, in particular, their strengths. One of our family activities revolves around this. Understanding our character strengths can help us help our children thrive. Currently, it's common to focus on the things going wrong – but it's our strengths that will really help us. They energise us and build our self-esteem.

Purpose

Since having a strong purpose will help us build our inner selves, the conversations in this section will help your family think about how to have a purposeful life, and in the world section, you will work towards a family mission that expresses your values, your desires and your purpose in life. Here are a few examples from my parents' survey to inspire you!

Sample Parents' Mission Statements

To grow myself out of a job.

- *To raise my children with honesty, transparency and vulnerability so that they have compassion and grace for others.*

- *To help my family work as a team, help each other reach our different potentials, and to love each other and others more each day.*

- *To let your kids create their own mission and be smart enough to know when to support, encourage or shut up and get out of the way!*

- *To give them the skills they need to be a valuable contributor to society and to find inner contentment.*

- *Facilitate hope and enthusiasm and a can-do/why-not attitude.*

- *Things always look much better in the morning.*

What's your purpose as a parent?

How would you like your family to find meaning and purpose?

What aspects of character will you need to encourage to get there?

Summary

We can help our children develop strong inner selves by helping them grow good definitions of what will really make them happy in life. By helping them give attention to their character and their meaning and purpose in life, we can help them weather whatever storms life throws at them.

Where there is hate, let me bring love
Where there is offense, let me bring pardon
Where there is discord, let me bring union
Where there is error, let me bring truth
Where there is doubt, let me bring faith,
Where there is darkness, let me bring light
Where there is sadness, let me bring joy

- Francis of Assisi

It is dangerous to go into eternity with possibilities which one has oneself prevented from becoming realities. A possibility is a hint from God. One must follow it.

- Soren Kierkegaard

CHAPTER 8

CONVERSATIONS FOR OUR INNER SELVES

Review the pre-activity notes for children at the end of the introduction before you begin the conversations. Grab notebooks and choose someone to read.

Where's My Soul?

 ## 1. Where we're headed

We're exploring what our soul is and how we can grow it, because it's vital to expanding our inner lives!

 ## 2. Packing our bags: what we need to know, or something to stimulate our thinking

If you lost your legs, would you still be you? Sure – so you're more than just your body. If you had an accident that damaged your brain, would you still be you? If you were all alone with no friends and family – you'd still be you. So, our soul helps us describe that part of ourselves that is more than body, mind and heart.

Our soul helps describe who we are, who we choose to be and the contributions we can make in the world. It's interested in good and evil and with the tiny little selfish or selfless decisions we make every day. Our soul is sometimes called spirit or conscience as it helps us choose which path to follow when our impulses might not be a great idea!

'Spirit' is often used to describe our strength or our character too. This might be the courage or wisdom we come up with in the face of danger or difficulty. Think of a horse that doesn't want to be tamed – we call it spirited. Someone who rescues another person has a heroic spirit or character. What makes some people more heroic than others?

Your soul is interested in the big questions of life. Research has found that all people are born with a need to connect to other people in relationships and to find meaning and purpose in their lives.[100] Happiness research says the same.

Spirit is also used when thinking about 'spiritual' or religious subjects. This is something that humans have been interested in throughout history.

My friend's son-in-law grew up in China. He said, 'We were taught in school that there was no such thing as God. I used to wonder why they had to teach us that. If there was no such thing, how come everyone kept wanting to know?'

3. Reading the map:
instructions or preparation

I was talking to a group of 12-year-old kids about spiritual issues a while ago. I asked them to name their biggest questions about life.

Drumroll please … The winner of the most popular question competition is:

What's the meaning of life?

Runner-up questions:

* Why are some people not as good as others?
* Why are there poor people?
* Why do some people have good health and some bad?
* Why can't I see God or talk to him?
* What happens to our souls after we die?
* Why isn't the world perfect?
* How does God help everyone?

These are all questions that are 'spiritual' or 'soulful' in nature.

Now it's your family's turn to think about your biggest questions and compare them.

What are your soul's questions? Write some down in your notebook before you chat.

4. On the road: our conversation

Greed, kindness, hope, pride, faith, peace, envy, mercy, fairness, honesty and humility are all 'soul' words. Can you think of more? Try to think of a time when someone in your family demonstrated one of these characteristics.

Think of someone you admire. Do you admire them for their spirit, strength, character or purpose? Describe that.

What soul characteristics do you like or dislike about yourself?

Different personalities find some soul characteristics easier than others. Maybe we are born with the possibility of all of them, but we can work on them to grow them or shrink them.

Sometimes our characters grow in us by watching our parents or others and copying them without even realising it.

Choose soulful words that describe your life now, as a formula: For example, someone feeling depressed or with poor self-esteem might say:

`my life now = (greed + envy) - (humility x hope)`

We all have plans and ideals for our life, but our soul is involved with how we are going to make our dreams happen.

Make a goal for your life by choosing the words that make up a sum of the life you'd like to have in the future (the ones you want and the ones you want to get rid of).

Example: `my future life = (courage + faith) - anger`

 # 5. Unpacking

Check in with each other about how you feel after this discussion.

Are you confused? Excited? Curious to know more? Uncomfortable?

Were you able to answer any of your spiritual questions?

(I think there are so many words to describe our inner selves because it's such a big and mysterious topic! At least, I'm a mystery to myself sometimes – are you?!)

6. Making the journey matter

Think of someone wise your family knows and take your spiritual questions to them.

You could also try praying – ask any spiritual question and see what happens!

What's My Superpower?

 ## 1. Where we're headed

To get a better idea of what our character strengths are and how we can use them to better our lives and others'!

 ## 2. Packing our bags: what we need to know, or something to stimulate our thinking

Morris Gleitzman, a popular author of books for kids, writes about hard stuff and what helps kids survive it. He reckons kids are heroic – and concerned for each other. While they may be small in size, what they think is big. Kids have great imaginations, which can help boost strength in difficult situations. They're also optimistic, and that can be very powerful.

Have you ever wondered why some people are more wise or brave? Why some people are more kind or humble? Some people are good at organising group activities or able to make people smile. What are your special superpowers?

Everyone has character strengths. How can we grow more of the best in humankind? Scientists have discovered 24 common strengths.[101] The same strengths are in every culture. They're divided into six categories: wisdom, courage, humanity, justice, temperance and transcendence.

We are nearly 10 times more likely to flourish if we know our character strengths and how to use them![102] They can grow our well-being and help us reach our goals in life. Since people have a natural tendency to remember negative things (we evolved like that so we can avoid danger), knowing our strengths balances us out a bit. They're like tools we take everywhere with us.

3. Reading the map:
instructions or preparation

Go to www.viacharacter.org/survey and register everyone in the family to take the free VIA survey, which takes about 15 minutes and tells you your greatest character strengths. Children under 13 need a parent to register them and there's a youth version.

By doing this, you'll also have participated in an ongoing study – so good on you!

4. On the road:
our conversation

Read through the top strengths your survey revealed. Write them in your notebook.

Do you like who they describe?

Share them with each other and see if your family members agree.

Imagine you're a superhero with these strengths. What name could your superhero have?

How would you use your special strengths to help people in the world?

For example, if forgiveness is one of your strengths, you could fly around the world helping people solve conflict by understanding each other's perspective. If curiosity is your strength, you might seek out new experiences or encourage others to learn; humour could help people get through difficult times with less stress, or if you are strong in kindness, you could fly around doing random acts of kindness to improve people's lives!

5. Unpacking

How do you already use your strengths? Brainstorm other ways you could use your strengths in your life – with relationships, or at school or work.

Explore the VIA Institute on Character. Their website resources have more ideas.

 # 6. Making the journey matter

Be inspired by these resources:

https://www.viacharacter.org/topics/articles/lets-get-serious-about-playing-with-our-strengths and more free games to learn about strengths can be found at https://www.allourstrengths.com/resources.

Here's a poster with all the strengths on it: https://www.viacharacter.org/pdf/Strengths%20by%20Virtue.pdf.

Love Beats Fear

 ## 1. Where we're headed

Understanding the relationships between hurt and anger and fear so we can find the courage to be loving people.

 ## 2. Packing our bags: what we need to know, or something to stimulate our thinking

My friend told me that when her son was five or six years old, they were talking about a problem and he said: "guess how sad I'm going to be when I finish being angry?" He understood that what was driving his anger was actually sadness. This was profound wisdom.

If you see someone who is angry, they probably feel either fear or hurt. When we feel afraid, our body's adrenalin kicks in and we feel a surge of strength ready to run or fight. This can come out as anger.

Similarly, if we feel afraid that someone doesn't love us, our body knows this is bad because being part of a caring tribe is important for our survival! In this way, love and fear are connected.

Anger is what we see on the outside, but there's something underneath driving it. Look for this something else. The trick is not to let negative emotions (like anger and fear) rule you. We can be more understanding or forgiving when we realise this about ourselves and others. And find reasons to be kind or grateful instead.

3. Reading the map:
instructions or preparation

* Think of someone you like. How do you feel?
* Now think of someone you don't like. How do you feel now?
* Now smile. A big smile. How do you feel?
* Think of someone who did something that made you angry.
* Now think of a time when you made someone else angry.
* Can your thoughts change your feelings?

4. On the road:
our conversation

* Describe a time you felt angry and work out whether hurt or fear was behind it?
* Imagine if you had smiled – what would be different?
* Is there anyone you would like to forgive?
* Who do you know who is good at loving people?
* What do they do that you could do too?

5. Unpacking

Is someone willing to share a time when they were angry with someone in your family? Can you gently talk together about it? What was the feeling underneath the anger?

Think of a code word to help remember to look for the fear or the hurt?

6. Making the journey matter

If I've convinced you that love beats fear, choose your love weapon of choice (smile, listen, understand, act kindly) and try it out!

How Would We Like to be Treated?

 ## 1. Where we're headed

To be more aware of the way we treat people so we can become kinder people.

 ## 2. Packing our bags: what we need to know, or something to stimulate our thinking

One of the most famous things Jesus Christ said was 'Do unto others as you would have them do unto you.' He was quoting from the oldest part of the Bible, which is also the Jewish holy book. This famous saying is found in most religions and cultures. It sounds simple, but it would have totally profound effects if we all actually lived by it!

Another way to say it is treat people the way you'd like to be treated. Sounds nice, huh? Lao Tsu, a Chinese philosopher, said, 'A wise person is good to people who are good. She is also good to people who are not good. This is true goodness.' This gets trickier, right?

 ## 3. Reading the map: instructions or preparation

This spiritual habit is so well known it has its own name – The Golden Rule. Can you think of some of its consequences in wider society? The legal or justice system for instance? What about at school or work?

Write a list of the ways you like to be treated.

4. On the road: our conversation

Here are some ways this habit could work out in our lives. Can you add more?

* Think of a time you did a good deed. How did it make you feel?
* Can you give up gossip for a day? (Don't say anything about someone that you wouldn't say to their face!)
* Think of something you need or would like and do it for someone else.
* Right a wrong. This may mean apologising to someone, returning something borrowed or trying to fix something you feel guilty about.

 # 5. Unpacking

Did anything come up that you want to change about how you treat each other in your family? At work or school? In your wider community?

 # 6. Making the journey matter

Try checking in with each other at dinnertimes about your practise of The Golden Rule.

Being Present

1. Where we're headed

To learn the useful habit of mindfulness so we can be present and aware – especially when life gets wild!

2. Packing our bags: what we need to know, or something to stimulate our thinking

I have trouble staying asleep. No problem going to sleep, but then I wake in the night for an hour or two! It drives me crazy! I've noticed that the busier my life is, the more often this happens. When I wake, my mind starts thinking about all sorts of things – processing the day's events, worrying about tomorrow's. My mind feels out of control, and I can feel emotionally exhausted. To combat this, I started listening to meditation apps on my phone to learn the skill of controlling my own thoughts. It was much harder than I expected, but it's starting to really work.

3. Reading the map: instructions or preparation

Can you pay attention to your thoughts? Are they realistic? Do they get you anxious? Do you speak to yourself kindly or harshly? Do you drift off when listening to others or can you concentrate?

You can learn the skill of mindfulness in many ways, because it's becoming widely studied and recommended. One reason for the interest in mindfulness is the way technology can interfere with being present and aware of others. The 'HeadSpace' app is a good introduction.[103] You could try researching a program or app, then the whole family could try it out for a week.

4. On the road: our conversation

Here are some ways we could practise this habit in our daily lives. Can you add more?

* For a whole day, only do one thing at a time. No multi-tasking! Give each activity your full attention. Try brushing your teeth with your other hand to help you concentrate on it.
* Pick one activity – like washing your hands or opening doors – and let it remind you of something important.
* Sit still and take a few deep breaths. You can make up something to repeat as you breathe – like smiling as you breathe in and relaxing as you breathe out.
* Try to focus on one part of your body at a time. Start with your toes and slowly work up to your head.
* Try praying. Shoot up chatty prayers to God. We used to pray when we came to a **STOP** sign: **S**orry, **T**hanks, L**O**ve and **P**lease (inserting appropriate things we're sorry about or grateful for, etc.).

5. Unpacking

Has anyone in your family already tried this habit? Have any of your friends? What ideas can you work on together? I'd especially recommend listening to the way you speak to yourself in your head. Perhaps you could write notes about this in your notebook this week.

Perhaps you could check in on each other about sleeplessness or anxiety and find a way to encourage this habit to see if it helps.

6. Making the journey matter

Sometimes the first evidence that mindfulness exercises are working for someone is that their family notices they are calmer, kinder, gentler. Keep an eye out on your family members as they try out this habit ☺

Watching for Spirit

 ## 1. Where we're headed

To learn to watch for the spirit of things: looking for the good in everyone. Warning: this is hard!

 ## 2. Packing our bags: what we need to know, or something to stimulate our thinking

There's a story about some religious men who lived and worked together. They mostly got along well, but as with all people, sometimes they argued about who was better, who was annoying and who should be the boss. An old wise man came to visit, and it was his job to care for these men and make decisions for them. Over his stay, they all came to him wanting to know who should be their leader?

To each enquirer, he suggested the name of a different man within the group. So at first, it looked like the wise man was making mischief. As the days passed, the men started deferring to each other, being kind and respectful to the man they thought would be their next leader. One day they realised the old wise man was gone, but the group was no longer in need of a leader.

If we all have a spirit, if we all feel love and fear and anger and grief, if we are all struggling along in this complex world, then it helps to remember that. We don't know what people are dealing with, but it helps everyone if we look for the good within them. Christians say this is seeing the image of God in everyone. It's an attitude shift that leads to a shift in our behaviour too.

If everyone has a spirit, then they all share something in common with you. It makes quite a difference to the way we treat people – whether we think they are basically good or basically bad. Looking for what is sacred in everyone and everything is the first step to finding it!

3. Reading the map: instructions or preparation

Almost everyone can teach us something. A kind person can inspire us to be kind. A mean person can teach us how bad that feels so we learn not to treat other people that way!

Pull out your notebooks and write a list of each member of your family and good friends. Then write down the name of someone you have a hard time liking.

4. On the road: our conversation

Here are some ways we could practise this habit in our daily lives. Using your list of people:

* Write down one thing about them that you think is good.
* Write down what you can do to be better at noticing their good traits.
* Think of someone you really respect or admire. How would you treat them if you saw them?
* For one day, try to treat everyone you meet in this same way. Watch what happens!

Can you add more ideas?

5. Unpacking

Try talking about the good characteristics of your family. Is there anything sacred about your family?

6. Making the journey matter

For the next day or so, try to see each person you meet as a teacher who has an important lesson for you!

Getting Wise

1. Where we're headed

To understand what's needed to make wise decisions so we can grow in wisdom.

2. Packing our bags: what we need to know, or something to stimulate our thinking

One of the hardest things in life is making good decisions. When I was young, I often had to choose between different things my divorced parents were telling me or asking me to do. Christmas was hard. I made some mistakes I still feel bad about. But I also knew deep down that some things were just wrong. Like Mum complaining to me about Dad. Dad never, ever complained about Mum, and I know now that he was wise.

One thing I've learnt is: I can choose to change some things. This is very important for helping to manage when hard things happen. We can choose our attitude if nothing else. I can choose how I respond. Will I be light-hearted or judgmental? Will I be accepting or upset?

It seems to me that some people are champions – they know how they want to change the world and they go and do it – not worrying too much about themselves in the meantime. They help people and inspire people. Other people, especially as they get older, just seem to think about themselves and their problems all the time, as if they are worse off than everyone else.

I know which one I want to be. What about you? The trick is to keep remembering this when we really do have problems. Sometimes the trick is like the serenity prayer:

God give me the serenity
to accept the things I can't change,
the courage to change the things I can,
and the wisdom to know the difference.

Serenity is a mixture of clearness and calmness, quietness and cool-ness, stillness and peace. No mental stress or anxiety. Sounds good, huh? One of the secrets to strength is attitude. You can ALWAYS change your attitude to things, even when you can't control things in your world.

When I was growing up, I couldn't change my parents being divorced and I couldn't stop my dad from drinking too much alcohol. In fact, when I tried (and I tried very hard), I just got miserable and couldn't get on with Dad at all. When I accepted it, knowing I'd tried all I could, I felt better. In the end Dad had to make the decision and I had to let go.

Courage is not just about being brave and strong. It's about changing things around you so you can make a difference. It's about choosing to do what's right even if it's hard. To do this, we need to learn to overcome our fear, our anger, our problems.

I often need the most courage when something goes wrong with someone in my family or with a close friend. I need a lot of courage to go and talk to them about it even if I feel hurt or angry, because otherwise it always just gets worse and worse.

Wisdom is about living life well. It often comes from our experiences, and it tells us how to use our knowledge. Sometimes it's even just knowing what's right in your gut. Knowing when you can change things in your world and when you can't is not easy, but you can always increase your wisdom.

Wisdom is different to information and knowledge. Knowledge is knowing that tomato is a fruit, wisdom is not putting it in fruit salad with ice cream! Wisdom is knowing the right or best way to be and act. The trick to being wise is to first realise when we're not! That humility is what makes us want to learn. So, you don't have to be old to be wise!

3. Reading the map: instructions or preparation

Think about these examples:

Courage: *My mum has inspired me heaps because she looked after my great-nanna when she was dying. She taught me to be strong and to keep your head up no matter if there is a challenge in life. Try and face it; don't back down – you can face it! (Kate, 13)*

Serenity: When bad things happen, I ...
* *Tell Mum (Jordan, 13)*
* *Scream into a pillow to let it out (Emily, 12)*
* *Dive in the water (Karl, 11)*
* *Let them go or sort out what went wrong and how it happened (Ashleigh, 10)*
* *Write them down and ask my friends for help (Astrid, 12)*

Wisdom: *A few years ago my friend Hanna who was older than me helped me get through a really hard time. Because of that, now I am helping a girl who is younger than me. I have become Hanna! Sometimes hard times make you wise enough to be a help to others. (Clare, 16)*

4. On the road: our conversation

Think about these four statements:

1. Life is amazingly precious.
2. Life is short and everyone dies eventually.
3. All lives contain some difficulties.
4. Our choices between right and wrong matter.

Now have a conversation using these prompts:

* Share your thoughts on these statements and the examples above together as a family.
* Share a time you were unwise.
* What are some of the things in your life that keep you from being fully happy that you just can't change? How might serenity help?
* What things might you need courage to change?

* What's the difference between being wise and being a know-it-all?
* Give a personal example about a hard thing you have been through in your life (big or small). What helped? What do you wish you'd done differently? What did you learn?

Experience is what you get when you didn't get what you wanted.

- Randy Pausch

 ## 5. Unpacking

Who is the wisest person in your family? Or are different people wise about different things?

Share what area you would like to become wiser in. How can you support each other as a family when you have hard decisions to make?

 ## 6. Making the journey matter

Ask someone you think is wise to recommend some wise writings you could read. Try to find some written for your age group. Or ask someone you think is wise if you could spend some time with them soon.

Spend a few minutes every day for the next week quietly alone in a beautiful place. Just let your mind wander on a deep question or something inspiring. Praying for wisdom is something we can always be confident about.

Keeping Calm

 ## 1. Where we're headed

In our busy and demanding culture, we can often get stressed or anxious. We can worry that we don't have the right things or that we don't have enough likes on Instagram. The number of people battling anxiety and depression is growing. Knowing how to keep our cool in a crisis or calm ourselves down when we're stressed are valuable skills that will help us stay true to our values, no matter what the world throws at us. This helps us cultivate serenity.

 ## 2. Packing our bags: what we need to know, or something to stimulate our thinking

Did you know: when you get a fright or something bad happens, your body chooses either FIGHT or FLIGHT. (Freeze is another option.)

Fight: you get angry and determined to defend yourself against any attack

Flight: you get fast and strong and prepared to run from danger

A hormone in your body, called adrenalin, starts to surge through you. It gives you almost superhuman strength for a little while. I read that mothers can even lift up cars to get their trapped babies out!

This is a good thing if you really are in danger. But in our daily lives, that's not so common (thank goodness). I haven't seen a bear or a lion in my suburb for ages. And despite the media coverage, fewer people get murdered now than in the 1940s!

But sometimes, you're just stressed. Maybe before a speech or when you think something nasty might happen to you. You don't need to run or fight then, so too much adrenalin is a problem. It stops digestion, for example. Too much adrenalin, for too long, wears your body out!

So we need to teach our bodies to relax. Very helpful before an exam – because you can't think well when you're not relaxed. Very helpful if you spend a lot of time worrying! And good for your happiness!

 ## 3. Reading the map: instructions or preparation

Relaxation companions:

* Exercise – gets rid of the adrenalin and gives you other hormones that make you feel happy instead!
* Drink more water – you really need lots of it!
* Do something you love – read, listen to music, hobbies.
* Write down your problems. This is a real help in sorting things out, expressing your fears/anger/worries and breaking them into achievable parts.
* Eat yummy stuff with a friend :o)
* Learn a relaxation exercise and practise it often.
* Breathe deeply – right into your belly!

Relaxation enemies:

* Lots of sugar. It hypes you up and then exhausts you. It also stops your body from fighting germs.
* Being too busy.
* Worry. We all need to learn to calm our minds. And worry doesn't actually fix anything.
* Technology – so many activities made to hype you up!

 ## 4. On the road: our conversation

Try this relaxation exercise. You can get very quick at this and use it anywhere, but it will take a little while to set up the first time.

Choose someone to read it out **slowly** as you all try.

Focus on your breathing for a few deep breaths and try to make your mind go blank.

Think of a landscape you really like – the beach, a creek, a forest, the snow, a desert maybe. Imagine you are there and have a good look around. Imagine the sounds and smells and your feelings.

Imagine you see a pathway. Follow it along, and imagine it brings you to a perfect spot to build a small cabin.

You decide to build your own special place there. Imagine a clearing. Maybe it has a nice view. Build a floor and some walls – use whatever materials you can dream up. It might be soft and feathery or bean-baggish, or it might be smooth timber or a crystal palace! Will the ceiling be clear so you can see the stars or covered with colourful scarves?

Now furnish your room. You can imagine any wonderful things you'd like to put in there! Scented candles? Cool music? Cuddly toys? This is your peaceful place that makes you smile just thinking about it. Maybe you will put familiar things, or maybe it will be a place where all your wishes exist! Make sure you put in a REALLY comfy place to sit.

Now that you're finished, just sit for a while and admire your creation!

When you've had enough time there, follow your pathway back out and return to reality. Are you refreshed and relaxed?

 ## 5. Unpacking

* Share something about your special place.
* Talk about when you might be able to use this.

 ## 6. Making the journey matter

If you practise this, you will be able to pop in to visit your perfect spot whenever you need to – at home, in the classroom, on a bus, at the top of a scary rollercoaster maybe?!!

There are loads of good apps for your phone to help you practise relaxation skills regularly.

Being a Generous Soul

 ## 1. Where we're headed

To become more generous so we can be happier and help others to be too.

 ## 2. Packing our bags: what we need to know, or something to stimulate our thinking

In our house, everyone knows the story of the pink plastic cups. I once went travelling in East Africa on the back of a truck. One day, we camped in a village in Malawi. While on a walk, I came across a church and talked to a lady there. She was an English teacher, and when her husband left her, the church let her live in one of the tiny concrete rooms with her baby. We spent the day together. I carried her baby on my back tied on with a piece of cloth. The next day, I went back for church, and the singing was amazing! I had a few spare Malawi money notes in my pocket, and I put them in the church collection bowl.

As I was about to say goodbye, I wondered how I could help this lovely lady. She asked me to wait as she went inside a little corner store. To my surprise, from this lady with nothing, I received a gift of two pink plastic cups. She said they were to remember Malawi by.

In a letter later, she told me that the church had never received notes before – only coins. I sent some money so she could buy a sewing machine. She gave some of it to the church to fix their roof. Those cups still teach me about generosity.

Wise people tell us that it is better to give than to receive. It doesn't always feel like that, but it's something that's worth trying. Helping others helps us be the best we can be. And, of course, it helps them too. And no one likes someone who is stingy!

3. Reading the map:
instructions or preparation

Generosity needs practise, though. We can start anywhere. When we learn to give willingly, we realise it feels good, so we do it again. Then giving becomes easier.

It also helps to believe that we live in a world where there is 'enough.' Advertisers want us to believe that there's not enough – *they say 'hurry and buy before they run out!'*

Imagine you have three jars. One for expenses (for play or bills to pay!); one for savings (for bigger or special things or for holidays), and one for gifts. Every week when you get pocket money or are paid for work, you need to choose how much money to put in each jar. Either choose a made-up amount or your real weekly income and decide how you will divide it.

Then think about who you might be generous towards with your gift jar. Many people pick 10 percent as a good starting amount for this jar. What could you do with that?

4. On the road:
our conversation

* Think of a chore that you do to help at home. Next time you do this chore, choose to see it as a generous act of service to others. Does it change how you feel about doing it?
* For one hour/day/week, count how many small acts of random kindness you can achieve.
* Start with a small thing that you'd like to be generous with and do it!
* Give someone a small gift – but do it anonymously! That helps to see whether we are being generous just to get people to like us!
* YouTube has so many inspirational stories about generous kids! Why not watch some together?

5. Unpacking

Decide as a family to give some money or food or help to others. Choose together how much the gift should be and whom to give it to. You might know someone who needs help, or you might decide to help an organisation that supports something important to you – animals, environment, refugees, the community work of your local church, kids with cancer … The list is long because so many people like to help! You may be doing it already!

 ## 6. Making the journey matter

Just do it! A great way to keep being generous is to set up a system (like a regular financial gift or a commitment to volunteer) so it becomes a habit rather than a feeling. Often the generosity of time helps ward off loneliness.

As Mahatma Gandhi said, 'Live simply, that others may simply live.'

Living a Purposeful Life

 ## 1. Where we're headed

Both happiness and resilience research suggest finding a purpose. We'll look at some ways to work out how we can find some purpose in our lives.

 ## 2. Packing our bags: what we need to know, or something to stimulate our thinking

Mark Twain, author of the great novel *Huckleberry Finn*, said, 'The two most important days of your life are the day you are born and the day you find out why.' Purpose tells us which direction to head in and how to spend our time. If we want to be a musician, this purpose tells us to head for lessons and to spend time practising. If we want to reduce plastic waste in the ocean, we'll talk to everyone about it, and ask our local cafés to stop using plastic straws.

Imagine a Venn diagram with three interconnecting circles. One circle is full of the things you like doing or are good at. One is the things you care about – saving puppies or being nice to lonely grandmothers. The third circle is full of the things the world needs – world peace, an end to extreme poverty, reduced carbon emissions (OK, and some smaller more local stuff like making a cake for school bake sale).

Your perfect purpose will be in the sweet spot that connects all three circles! Don't worry – it might take a while to find it, and it can change over the course of your life – but it's a great goal!

Purpose is important for leaders of big organisations and for little people leading themselves. Purpose can be in the future – what you intend to do. It can get you out of bed in the morning and it can help produce your actions now. It can lift your spirits and give meaning to your life. Purposeful people keep going when the going gets tough, and they don't worry about little things on the way. Perhaps you know the feeling of being totally absorbed in a project – in the zone? That's why purpose makes us happier and more resilient. Some purposes are shared with others, and others are ours alone.

 # 3. Reading the map: instructions or preparation

Draw three big interconnecting circles in your notebook. Start filling them each with answers to these three questions.

1. What do you love doing or people say you're really good at?
2. What do you feel strongly about – what do you care about or what makes you mad?
3. What things in the world would you like to improve in your lifetime?

Read this little George Bernard Shaw quote and answer the questions below.

This is the true joy in life, the being used for a purpose recognised by yourself as a mighty one; the being thoroughly worn out before you are thrown on the scrap heap; the being a force of nature instead of a feverish selfish little clod of ailments and grievances complaining that the world will not devote itself to making you happy.[104]

* Do you agree or not?
* Do you know any people like the ones described here?
* Which type is more attractive?
* What would you like to be a force of nature about?

 # 4. On the road: our conversation

Share your circles with each other. Encourage one another or ask questions to help them dig deeper into their purpose. Converse with each other to help you each create your purpose.

One way to think about purpose is to ask: What matters to you? What matters most?!

We can easily get too busy or distracted and forget to make purposeful time for what (or who) really matters to us.

What do you do in your family to be purposeful about building your relationships with each other? (Hint: you're doing something right now!)

Another way to think about purpose is to know 'why' you want to do things. Keep asking why until you get to the deepest purpose. Kids are great at asking why!

 ## 5. Unpacking

Mother Theresa said, 'It's not what you do, but how much love you put into it that matters.' When people are dying, they don't say they wish they spent more time working or getting awards. They wish they'd shown more love and been more true to themselves.

Are you being true to yourself and your purpose?

How does this work with all the things that have to be done – like homework or cooking or earning money to live? These can all be seen as purposeful too - or as chores. Does it make a difference?

Check in with each other if you're not sure. Check whether anyone is feeling frustrated or lost or still wondering where to start searching for their purpose.

 ## 6. Making the journey matter

Interview some older friends or family about their purpose. For example, ask them what they really care about or what causes they support. Ask them what kept them going when the going got tough?

CHAPTER 9

CARING ABOUT OUR WORLD

Little kids are born very focused on themselves; they have to be – it's a survival thing. So, when they need something, they make a lot of noise to get it. Some people don't grow out of this, I admit, but most people become aware of the wider world around them. Our world starts small – just our family – but then the world grows to preschool and then school and high school, and then to the big world of work. Somewhere in there, we learn about the universe. How big is the universe? How big are you in relation to that? Kind of makes sense that the universe is not centred around you or me, doesn't it?

Do you know anyone who thinks they are the centre of the universe? Not pleasant to be around are they?! At some point, we all need to choose to focus on other people and on things more significant than us. To think about how people can exist on a planet together peacefully, as well as how a family can exist in a house together peacefully! My dad says a good rule of thumb is to imagine what would happen if everyone did it.

1. How are we going now?

Harvard University's report 'The Children We Mean to Raise: The Real Messages Adults are Sending about Values' surveyed 10,000 diverse young people.[105] They found that on the youth survey, only 20 percent ranked 'caring for others' above achievement or happiness – they valued their personal success over caring for others.

The researchers found a disconnect when they surveyed the parents though. A full 96 percent of the parents said they wanted to raise ethical, caring children. They even cited the development of moral character as 'very important, if not essential'. What went wrong, then? Why don't the young people's results match this? Because 80 percent of the youths surveyed also reported that their parents 'are more concerned about achievement or happiness than caring for others'. Their parents' intentions didn't match their actions, and they modelled it. Simply thinking about compassion is not enough.

Actions count. The United Nations' Millenium Development Goals inspired action and did a great job of raising children out of poverty around the world from 2000 to 2015.[106] But there are now nearly 80 million people around the world who have been forced to flee their homes because of conflict or disaster. That's more than 1 in every 100 people on Earth. That, along with the combined effects of the coronavirus, are catastrophic. We had mothers and fathers already struggling to feed their children. Sons and daughters already missing out on an education. People already unable to get the basic medical care we take for granted. And then a pandemic on top. With all that going on, many of our gains in reducing extreme poverty are set to be reversed.

Knowing that there is much still to be done, why is it that we don't take more compassionate action? Two reasons come to mind: sometimes, our privilege can actually be standing in the way, and we don't realise that reducing poverty isn't just about giving to those in need; it's also about knowing what is enough for ourselves. When I went to look at development projects in one of the poorest countries in the world, it was winter in Nepal. It has the highest mountains, and it gets pretty cold! I took feather jackets, waterproof shoes, thermals – everything I could get my hands on – because I hate the cold. For three weeks, I walked around with my feet like ice blocks. I missed my family, the travel was difficult, but the development projects were inspirational. I tried not to complain, but I found it hard. Until one day when we drove past a mountain river full of women barefoot in the water washing clothes. Impossible to complain after that. I'd been to Nepal 20 years earlier as a hip young trekker, but this time, I recognised my privilege.

I continually try to recognise my privilege, as one of my jobs was helping people understand issues of poverty and injustice. I wrote and spoke about what a difference great development could make in the lives of people in such difficult circumstances. We've come a long way in the last 20 years. **I think we understand now that generosity to the poor is a good thing. A much harder message, though, is that we, in developed countries, need to learn how much is enough.** Imagine if we were to give generously to the poor around the world so they could live like a middle-class American or Australian. We would end up needing three planets to sustain us, because we go through a lot of resources!

If, however, everyone in the world were to live like a middle-class Westerner did in 1970, we would need only one planet – perfect. The implication of this for me is that continuous economic growth is not sustainable. What we need is to find some level of 'enough' that brings us contentment and sustainability. This led me to look at the effects of consumerism in our society, and specifically, the effects on children.

I live in one of the richest countries on the planet. Yet Clive Hamilton, in his book *Affluenza*,[107] points out that when Australians were asked whether they can afford to buy everything they really need, nearly two-thirds said no. Yet, in the annual 'Global Wealth Reports' done by Credit Suisse, they list Australia as the second richest county in the world,[108] with Norway as the richest (I'd rather have beaches than snow), so we're doing pretty well.[109] If we don't realise that, though, we will never find contentment – we'll never feel like we have enough. And many others will not even have enough to live.

The earth is here to share and sharing needs kids who care!

In summary, we are doing worse than we were before, as many of our efforts have been reversed. Too many of us let our privilege and our inability to see what is enough stand in our way of taking compassionate action.

2. What can we imagine would be better?

When my children were in primary school, I introduced them to Tearfund's 'Really Useful Gift Catalogue'. You can buy a goat for $50 that will be given to someone who really needs it. Anyway, I'd told them about children in Africa and children in Southeast Asia and the struggles that they had. I also told them about the inspirational work that was done to help people help themselves. Tearfund's gift catalogue is an easy-to-understand way to show how little it costs to help.[110]

That afternoon my kids came to me and told me that they had added up how much it would cost to buy one of everything in the gift catalogue, and it came to $5,500. They told me they would like to raise enough money to buy one of everything. They'd been inspired by an ABC video that I'd shown them about a boy who had found out about children in Africa who didn't have enough clean water. He'd done chores around the house and inspired his friends to raise enough money to buy a well for a village. I guess they wanted to do something similar.

To my shame, my first thought was, 'My goodness that's too much – they'll never be able to achieve that! They need some kind of goal they can realistically meet.' I didn't say that out loud, of course! Instead, we brainstormed how they could raise the money. I suggested that they write letters to members of their family that give them birthday and Christmas presents. They wrote letters asking if this year they could have a gift from the gift catalogue rather than a present for themselves. Well, my gift-giving extended family rose to the occasion, and they were very generous that year!

My boys went three years without Christmas presents or birthday presents. Their parents were very generous to Tearfund over those years, and I'm extremely proud to tell you that they met their goal. I had children at their school trying to hand me five dollars saying, 'This is my lunch money. Could you give it to some poor children, please?' In my experience, kids don't need to have generosity and compassion and empathy instilled in them. They need to be given opportunities to practise it.

This made me think parenting is like a dance. I raised awareness for my children of the plight of other children in the world … they came up with an idea. I helped them work out how they could put that idea into practise … they did the work. I encouraged them along the way. A bit of thought for me, a bit of input from them, and this dance of parenthood created a sense of identity and purpose in my children. They became world-changers!

Too often we provide our children with adult solutions to some of the world's problems, or don't talk about them at all. Rather, we could present them with the issue at hand and invite their suggestions for what we could do. The world is filled with stories of children today who are changing their community and the world in their own way. What might your children be capable of if they were given the opportunity?

In summary, we need to teach compassionate action to ourselves and give opportunities for our children to practise their inherent compassion.

3. What can we change to get there?

What do you think is one of the biggest addictions we use daily that is legalised, subsidised and even distributed to children? In *Humankind: A Hopeful History*, Rutger Bregman says we're hooked on the nightly news despite the side effects that are found to cause 'a misperception of risk, anxiety, lower mood levels, learned helplessness, contempt and hostility towards others and desensitization'.[111] We think we are being good citizens by watching the news, but Bregman says studies are showing that it's a mental health hazard. I've been talking about this for years without knowing the research. The problem is that the news highlights exceptional negative events, so we get a skewed understanding of what's wrong in the world and how frightened we should be. And this paralyses our compassion.

Understand the real state of the world

Hans Rosling was a hugely charismatic man with a passion for saving children and for dispelling ignorance to that end.

His life work culminates in a book I've just read that I'm now hugely passionate about – *Factfulness: Ten Reasons We're Wrong about the World – and Why Things Are Better Than You Think.*[112] In his words:

> *This book is my last battle in my lifelong mission to fight devastating ignorance. It is my last attempt to make an impact on the world: to change people's ways of thinking, calm their irrational fears, and redirect their energies into constructive activities. Previously I armed myself with huge data sets, eye-opening software, an energetic learning style and a Swedish bayonet for sword-swallowing. It wasn't enough. But I hope this book will be.*

Hans sets out to show how we make mistakes with our overly dramatic instincts and worldviews. And from this, we instinctively make decisions that are unhelpful or even untrue. These can have devastating consequences. Hans tries to turn us towards a fact-based worldview instead. I don't want to spoil the surprise for the family activity coming, so I won't say much here. The good news is that we are already making a difference and research is getting clear about what things help the most. So we can do more of them!

Reduce environmental damage

Hans Rosling shows that the world's population will level out.[113] One of the direct results of educating impoverished women is they have fewer children. In fact, women who have already been pulled out of extreme poverty will have fewer grown-up children in the next couple of decades. These children will have less impact on the world's resources than children from higher-income families. This means those of us who are in the top 10 percent of world income (most of us in Australia and America) can actually have the most impact by reducing our materialistic waste.

A 2020 study argues that in order to help the world today, simply relying on new technologies won't be enough.[114] These scientists show that 'the world's top 10% of income earners are responsible for between 25 and 43% of environmental impact.' In contrast, 'The world's bottom 10% income earners exert only around 3–5% of environmental impact.' Therefore, lifestyle change for those of us who are wealthy resource-guzzlers is going to be crucial. An atmospheric scientist at Penn State University, Professor Michael Mann, was reported in an article as saying, 'What COVID-19 has laid bare is the fragility of this massive infrastructure which we've created to artificially maintain consumption far beyond the natural carrying capacity of the planet.'[115]

Learning to reduce our desires to 'we have enough' is not an easy sell. I know – I've tried. I can barely manage it in my own life. We have solar panels and a hybrid electric car. We buy second-hand clothes and have reduced our meat consumption. But I'm forever getting stuck on some new gadget in a Facebook ad! We need to do it for our children and their children, though.

The good news is that children prefer spending time with their parents to having new stuff anyway. So we can give our children more life experiences and more time with friends and community. And bonus, we can opt to invest in generosity during those life experiences and time spent together. This makes a memorable life experience for both us and the receiver. Helping other people reach above the minimum threshold of poverty will actually make both of us happier![116]

To really help others, we'll need to realise that wealth isn't just about money, and overseas aid organisations don't want us to just give money – they need us to change our lifestyles too.

Give love and aid to charitable organisations

We feel most alive when we love and are loved back. So we need to give love, not just money. Charitable organisations' newsletters are full of stories of real people who are making change. They're hoping to work against the insulating effect of wealth to increase our empathy and compassion for others. Empathy is most useful if it leads to a response. Generosity is a simple response to the injustice we see around us in the world.

We have also impoverished ourselves if we don't understand the effects of poverty on one's soul. Poverty is a holistic problem. When people are isolated or excluded (through discrimination) from access to resources, their security and self-esteem are undermined. Shame and disrespect lead to vulnerability and ill-health, and a cycle of despair ensues. This psychological aspect to poverty, when peace and hope are gone, is the most insidious and difficult to remedy. Giving people skills to help themselves rebuilds this confidence.

Good aid organisations also raise awareness of structural injustices, encourage action in powerful countries and strengthen local government systems. They provide advocacy training to encourage people to bring about change themselves, ensuring their projects provide sustainable and holistic development. These include hospitals and income-generation opportunities. Education helps too, from road safety to childcare to scholarships. Food security projects bring better seeds and kitchen gardens; others care for orphans and widows. Many challenges exist, and the approach is slow, but it is empowering, effective, sustainable and transformational.

When I visited a women's group in Nepal, I saw how generous donations are efficiently spent. Eighteen women dressed in red greeted us atop a hill with garlands and clapping. We heard how these women became a self-help women's group one and a half years ago, with the help of a local non-government organisation (NGO). They discussed women's health issues, they organised sanitation and toilets, and they taught the women to read and write. Their next step was to build a community centre. They had collected money, cleared a site and were negotiating with the local council for the rest of the budget.

Before the NGO formed their group, these women had been shy and frightened. They'd married into strange villages at very young ages, illiterate and alone. Some couldn't even sign their name, but the NGO helped them gain this dignity. Over and over they told us they have more voice in the village now that they are united. They'd been provided kitchen garden training and the ladies produced a variety of vegetables year-round, rather than one vegetable that lasted only nine months of the year. Even the men helped out in the garden now – revolutionary!

One month before, a woman was killed by her husband. This whole women's group marched to the district police to advocate for punishment as domestic violence had previously been ignored. Some of the women educate others, and they are at last seeing a decline in ignored domestic violence. They've also noticed more equality for their daughters. They ask their sons to help with the work now, and families are sending their daughters to school with their sons.

When we visited with them, there was plenty of laughter, chat and smiles amongst this group of newly empowered women cooing over each other's babies. We asked them how they wanted their daughters' lives to be different. They responded quickly that they wanted them to be educated, independent and able to marry whomever and whenever they chose. Women full of hope are a powerful force. All this was achieved with no money given to the women. Instead, the money was used to pay the local wage of a community development worker who encouraged and equipped them. **This was enough to dramatically increase the likelihood of the village lifting itself out of debilitating poverty.**

Become an advocate

Imagine a teenage boy in a new high school. He's been picked on and now is in his first fight. Through his panic and the crowd, he spots his much bigger brother. Just watching. The pain he feels at his brother's lack of help – his lack of advocacy – lasts decades. The brothers are now estranged.

Advocacy, standing up for someone else, starts with anger and compassion at injustice, but it leads to hope. In his book about advocacy called *Just Speak*, master advocate Scott Higgins says:

> *We refuse to accept a world where injustice, alienation and poverty mar life. We dream that things can be different, and having dreamed that dream, we set about working with God to call it into being.*[117]

It's a bold and beautiful vision. I'm attracted to and therefore decided to follow the teachings of Jesus because this is his vision. He called for care for women and children, for the poor and sick and marginalised. Inspired by the teachings of Jesus, both Gandhi and Martin Luther King Jr. led successful non-violent advocacy campaigns.

Advocacy works. People challenged tobacco companies and whale hunters and won. A recent advocacy example is The Ethical Fashion Guide produced by Baptist World Aid. Their team surveys hundreds of fashion brands each year, asking questions about fair wages and a range of ethical metrics. Then they track changes corporates make. From this information, they produce a booklet with grades that shoppers can use to decide how to buy ethical fashion. These shoppers tell their friends and run 'Clothes Swap' events to raise awareness. There is consistent growth in the number of corporate fashion brands conceding to consumer pressure for fairer worker treatment. Modern Slavery Acts have been passed around the world after advocacy actions.

Advocacy is used as strategic development work around the world. Communities are encouraged to advocate for themselves in their local situations. Children advocate against child marriage using street theatre in Nepal. Children's rights are championed in Malawi through mobile rural courts. Trained children advocate for better health by visiting homes in Bangladesh. And children around the world hit the streets to advocate for action on climate change.

If we want a better world, we need to teach, support and help our kids to be advocates.

Advocate for compassion

Often advocates are born out of tragedy. I think of parents who have lost children to drugs or to gun violence who then become powerful advocates for education and change. Brené Brown in *Rising Strong as a Spiritual Practice* says:

> This is the definition I use for compassion: Recognizing the light and dark in our shared humanity, we commit to practicing loving kindness with ourselves and others in the face of

suffering. This is the struggle with compassion. Compassion is not a default response, because in order to practice compassion, you have to be able to recognize the darkness in you and in other people.

It's often the parts of ourselves that have been wounded that bring healing to others. Our wounds – our pain, our mistakes – help us have compassion for the wounds of others. Only when we recognise our own weakness do we have space to be gracious to the weakness of others. When we've been lonely or scared or sad, we can recognise it in the face of others and need not turn away. By recognising it, we can empathise. Essentially, it helps us help. I am present when people face loss because I remember what I needed when I lost my sister. I can sit with people who are depressed because I've been down and know it will pass, but it's lonely.

It's also the wounds of people I know and love that give me this empathy. My advocacy career began when I had small children. I learnt that my government was locking up small children when their families sought asylum. I was horrified. I got involved with an organisation raising awareness. We took our kids on marches. Strong grassroots advocacy from parents and children got all those children out of immigration detention!

But it wasn't until we accepted an asylum seeker into our home that I really found purpose. I walked with him through crazy paperwork and cried with him about his lost family. I took him for driving tests and bought plants for him to grow. We saw our broken culture through his eyes. He became an uncle to our sons. Then I realised that immersing myself in helping even one person could also change the world. Sometimes that's all we've got.

Edmund Burke said *'The only thing necessary for the triumph of evil is for good men to do nothing.'* **Advocacy is good people doing something!** I'm hoping you and your family will find the causes you want to advocate for as you play with the next family conversations.

Summary

The news can give us a skewed perspective of the world. So to help the world, we first need to know what state it is truly in. Then we need to do our part to reduce environmental damage. As we strive to help those who are less fortunate, we need to remember the power of love and enabling people to help themselves. Become an advocate for someone or join a cause and always advocate for compassion for people around you.

'Never doubt that a small group of thoughtful, committed citizens can change the world. Indeed, it is the only thing that ever has.'

- Margaret Mead.

Won't it be a great day when schools have all the money they need and the air force has to have a cake stall to buy a bomber.

- Would you believe I saw it on a tea towel?

CHAPTER 10

CONVERSATIONS FOR OUR WORLD

Review the pre-activity notes for children at the end of the introduction before you begin the conversations. Grab notebooks and choose someone to read.

Our Worldviews

1. Where we're headed

To understand a bit more about how we see the world, or our 'world-views'. Understanding your worldview allows you to consider where you fit in and what contribution you can make!

2. Packing our bags: what we need to know, or something to stimulate our thinking

Different people around the world have different 'worldviews'. It's a collection of our beliefs about the world and our place in it. Or it's the story that we live by.

We form our worldview as children, so perhaps you'd better give it some thought!

Imagine asking 1,000 4- to 14-year-old kids what they worry about. Most kids worry most about bullying, then war, then the environment and child poverty. It's interesting that these are not small self-centred things. Were they similar to your worries?

When kids are asked who inspires them to make a better world, the highest response is Mum and Dad, then friends and then God. Other family members and teachers rate higher than any famous people.

Nearly 9 out of 10 kids think that they could make their life and the world around them a little or a lot better. Being kind and volunteering to help others are the main ways they think they could do this, as well as giving money to charity and recycling. What do you think?

Professor James Sire wrote a helpful book called *The Universe Next Door*. It says we can know a bit about a person's worldview by the way they answer four questions.[118]

1. **Who am I?** (what are people like and what am I supposed to do as a human?)
2. **Where am I?** (what's the world like? is it ordered or random?)
3. **What's wrong?** (why are some things just not right?)
4. **What's the solution?** (what's the hope for things to get better?)

3. Reading the map: instructions or preparation

Some people have a worldview that says we are all here by chance and that life is random. Would this influence how they might respond to helping other people?

Others have a worldview that says people are a mixture of good and bad and life is a struggle between those different impulses. Does this feel true for you?

Some have a worldview that there is a God in charge and helping us help each other. How might this affect people who believe or who don't?

Another worldview is that what we do in this life makes a difference for us in the next life.

My worldview is one of the reasons I've written a book about raising kids who care. My worldview inspires people to care for each other in a world that has enough for us all to share. When we don't share, that's unfair to some people, and the solution is to get more people to care!

Here are a couple of statements that hint at worldviews. Thinking about the four questions, what do you think their worldviews might be?

I think the world needs more people willing to sacrifice themselves for the greater good. (Angus, 14)

Something I think is really great is that we have the chance to help other people in the world who are struggling (Michael, 12)

4. On the road: our conversation

So what are your answers to the four big questions?

1. people are …
2. the world is …
3. bad things in the world are …
4. things could get better if …

Discuss these with your family.

 # 5. Unpacking

*   What worries you about the world?
*   Who inspires you?
*   Does your whole family have a similar worldview?
*   What could you do as a family to make things better in the world?

 # 6. Making the journey matter

Can you create a conversation for one of the issues that worries you?

There's a blank template at the end of this book you can use.

How is the World Going?

 ## 1. Where we're headed

To get a realistic idea of the state of the world so we know best how and where to contribute.

 ## 2. Packing our bags: what we need to know, or something to stimulate our thinking

One of the best books I've ever read is *Factfulness* by Hans Rosling. The book starts with a short quiz asking simple questions about global trends in poverty, population, and education. He's asked CEOs and academics and audiences these questions for years.

Don't go on until your whole family has taken the quiz. My prediction is that it will be very surprising, and that kids will do better than adults!

You can take the test at https://www.gapminder.org/test/. It will only take about five minutes.

 ## 3. Reading the map: instructions or preparation

Literally no one ever gets near passing this test! Worse – we are negative in our responses – less than a chimpanzee making chance guesses! We see doom and gloom everywhere. *Factfulness* tells us why, psychologically, this is true and what to do about it. It shows how little people really realise about the improved state of our world, and what simple steps we need to take to improve this.

Factfulness is the stress-reducing habit of only carrying opinions for which you have strong supporting facts. It helps because we can focus on what the data shows really works and be encouraged by the life-saving progress we've made in the past.

Hans is very encouraging about the state of the world and lists many of the things that have improved in the world in the last century. We've had huge increases across the globe in women's right to vote, protection of nature, new music and films, science scholarship and cereal yields, literacy and democracy.

We want everyone to have access to the world's resources that they need to flourish in life. A great way to think about what we want to achieve is to imagine three people trying to peer over a fence at a show. They find three similar boxes to stand on to help. If they want equality, they get one each, but imagine the people are all different heights. The tallest person doesn't even need the box to see, the box helps the middle one to see, but the shortest still can't see over the fence even on the box.

If we aim for equity rather than equality, then if the tallest person gives the shortest their box as well, all three can easily see over the fence. Unfortunately, reality says the tallest has lots more boxes than they need and the shortest is down in a ditch.

Our amazing planet has enough capacity to feed everyone in the world. The issue is always how we share it.

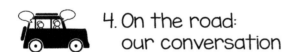 # 4. On the road: our conversation

Talk about your results on the quiz.

* What surprised you?
* Which questions or issues are you most concerned about?
* Watching the news gives us an idea about what state the world is in. Is this an accurate measure? How might the news change our view of what is common or uncommon? Why doesn't the news report more good news?

5. Unpacking

Investigate how you could get involved in helping with the issue that you most care about as a family. You could start with the issues raised by the questions in the quiz.

Next time you watch the news, can you make an effort to watch for the ways people are helping? In a car accident, is there an ambulance saving people? After a natural disaster, who is helping clean up? Are there people or organisations providing food and shelter?

How might this make you feel differently?

 ## 6. Making the journey matter

Hans Rosling was a wonderful presenter and has given many inspiring talks. You could watch one or two together here: https://www.ted.com/playlists/474/the_best_hans_rosling_talks_yo.

Another great place to explore what's really going on in the world is https://ourworldindata.org/. They answer questions about how we spend our time, work and energy with colourful graphs!

Understanding Poverty

 ## 1. Where we're headed

To understand a bit more about how different people live in the world.

 ## 2. Packing our bags: what we need to know, or something to stimulate our thinking

There are some kids just like you around the world who will never read this book. These kids laugh like you, love like you and have desires like yours. But they are unlikely to have much influence over their own lives, let alone anyone else's. Maybe they didn't get to go past primary school before they had to go to work to help their family.

Would you extend your influence to those who don't have the same privileges and power as you so they can have a chance to be the best they can be too?

There are some big problems in our world. Many people think they're too big to do anything about. But there have always been people who have proved them wrong. There are loads of good things being done in the world to help everyone flourish.

 ## 3. Reading the map: instructions or preparation

Which of these kids sounds most like you?

* Hi, my name's Francis, and I live in Africa. I'm in year 6, and I live with my mum and three brothers. My dad has been very sick, and we don't have much money because we had to sell some of our land to pay for his medicine.

* Hi, my name's Kate, and I live in Australia. I am in year 5 and our family of four lives in a house with 14 rooms. I had a cold this winter, so we had some extra vitamin C and lots of strawberries.

* Hi, my name's Vincent, and our family lives on the money Mum earns working in the sugar cane fields. She earns $3.50 per day. It costs us $1.75 per day to buy corn for our whole family to eat.

* Hi, my name's Sam, and my mum looks after us kids while Dad goes to work in the city. He earns $180 per day, and after Mum goes shopping at the supermarket, we spend about $45 per day on our food, so we have quite a bit left over. This Christmas we're going on a holiday to Queensland! We've bought lots of mozzie repellent, so we don't get itchy bites.

* Hi, my name's Maureen. My sisters and I get bitten with mozzies whenever we go to the spring to collect the water. I carry it on a big bucket on my head. Every year we all get sick with malaria. My little brother died from it last year.

* Hi, my name's Oliver. At home it's my job to unstack the dishwasher. I do it when Dad reminds me. I also have to take the recycling out to the bin on Thursday nights. I feel bad if I forget and Mum has to do it for me.

* Hi, my name's Eunice. I get up at 5 a.m. every day to walk to the forest for firewood. It takes me and my sister 40 minutes to get there. We chop the branches, bundle them together, and carry the heavy loads home on our heads. Then we can light a fire to boil water for our breakfast. If we don't boil it we get sick.

* Hi, my name's Mark. We have a microwave and a fridge and a stove and a kettle and a toaster and lights and taps and a sink and a pantry in our kitchen.

* Hi, my name's Daniel. No one in our village has electricity, but one person has a telephone. We don't have a toilet. We have to go out to the bushes at night and the mozzies bite our bottoms.

* Hi, my name's Naomi. This year I read a funny book by John Marsden called *Staying Alive in year 5*.

* Hi, my name's Lydia. Only 7 out of 10 children make it to year 5 alive in Kenya.

4. On the road: our conversation

The problem with poverty is that it's just not fair! But it's fixable. The kids from Kenya in these stories are real. The organisation *Tearfund* raises money to help them with new toilets and a worker to provide the extra information they need.

The cool thing about these kids is that they learnt to make their lives, and even their whole village, better. They learnt how to protect themselves easily from mozzies and disease, and how to make water clean. Then they taught their families.

Poverty affects all of life – it changes the way you feel about yourself. So helping people feel hopeful and that there's something they can do to change things makes a big difference.

If you think about the people where you live, do you think you are rich or poor?

If you think about the whole world, does that change?

Brainstorm ways your family could help kids who haven't had the same opportunities as you.

Look up https://www.kiva.org/ for very specific ways you could help people around the world. Kiva lets you lend someone as little as $25 towards their small-business idea (it's like crowdfunding). You can choose who, where and what causes you'd like to support with your money. You can also choose to withdraw the loan when it's repaid or to reinvest it in someone else who needs it. (I just read about someone who has made her 11th loan to single mothers in Nicaragua). It has great specific people and stories you can read about. Choose one together!

5. Unpacking

How did you feel reading about the kids in Kenya?

Does it make you want to do something to help?

Actually doing something concrete will help you overcome just feeling sad or guilty. That's the problem with just watching news stories about bad things in the world – they can make you feel helplessly sad or even guilty that your life is so great!

How did you feel after reading about the people on kiva.org?

 ## 6. Making the journey matter

My son's class acted out the stories above in a school assembly. It was his idea to contrast the two groups like that. You can learn more about them in the 'Kaborogin Kids Lead the Way' Kids4Kids pack on the Tearfund website https://www.tearfund.org.au/. Or you could ask someone new to your country about the place they've come from.

Being Part of the Solution

 ## 1. Where we're headed

Thinking about actions we can take to encourage others to make a difference in the world too – by raising money to help or by raising awareness of an issue through hosting an activity.

 ## 2. Packing our bags: what we need to know, or something to stimulate our thinking

My children watched a video called *Ryan's Well* about a Canadian boy who heard that kids in Africa didn't have access to clean water. Ryan worked extra jobs for four months to earn the $70 he thought it cost to build a well. Then he discovered he'd misunderstood, and it was more like $1,000! He didn't give up – he encouraged others to pitch in until he had enough. He just kept going, and lots of people were inspired to help.

Eventually, he was able to visit the village he'd helped so much. It was awesome what that one kid had done. **Ryan was only seven years old when he did this.** Today if you visit https://www.ryan-swell.ca/, you'll see he has a foundation that has helped over a million people have access to clean water! You can watch a video about his story there too.

Well, after seeing this, my kids wanted to do something too. They decided to raise enough money to buy one of everything in a gift catalogue called 'Arguably the World's Most Useful Gift Catalogue'. You can buy a goat or a mosquito net or a year's primary schooling and give a card to someone you know. Their present has actually gone to someone overseas who really needs it. They calculated that one of everything would cost $5,500.

My boys wrote to all their relatives that might give them Christmas presents and asked them to give from the catalogue instead. Everyone in our extended family was inspired and bought these gifts for everyone. It took three years (and their parents were extra generous those years!), but the boys achieved their goal by being prepared to sacrifice their own gifts and by inspiring others.

Pretty cool huh? Heaps of the other families at their school joined in then too.

3. Reading the map: instructions or preparation

There are many organisations that help you raise money as you experience a little of what others endure. I did the World Vision 40-Hour Famine once. It was awful. I got so hungry – and I get grumpy when I'm hungry. But the tricky thing about it is you can't complain. Every time you get hungry (and it happens a lot over 40 hours), you remember that people all over the world feel like this all the time. That's the point really. It's amazing how understanding how someone else feels makes you want to help them.

4. On the road: our conversation

You could do the Famine, or you could just try it for a day anyway. You don't even need to stop eating completely. Try for one day as a family:

* going without anything sweet
* going without electricity
* collecting water from one tap in your house in a big pot and using it every time you need water in a day

Or, if you're feeling really wild, you could give a dinner (or just an afternoon tea), which would make a real impact on your visitors. You're going to serve different types of food at random - based on what ticket they get as they arrive at your door. The tickets will make them rich, middle class, or poor for the rest of the meal.[119] You could do it at home with just your family and some invited friends. (We did it at church and invited lots of people and charged them to raise money too.)

You'll need to invite at least six people and give them one of three different coloured 'tickets' as they arrive, e.g., blue = rich, yellow = middle, red = poor.

If you have 6 people, there would be 1 rich, 4 middle and 1 poor. If you have 30 people, there would be 5 rich, 20 middle and 5 poor. These are the approximate distributions in the world.

	Afternoon Tea Menu:	Dinner Menu:
Rich:	packet of chocolate biscuits	a take-away meal
Mid:	fruit salad	vegetable curry and rice
Poor:	a small carrot stick	a bit of rice

It's really interesting to collect the rubbish each group uses too. The rich ones make a big mess!!!

 ## 5. Unpacking

How did your guests react? Did the poor group get angry? Did the rich feel guilty? Did anyone share across the groups?

Which of these appeals to you most?

* Help care for animals
* Protect the environment
* Volunteer to help others
* Give money to charity
* Practise random acts of kindness
* Take part in events that are organised by others to raise money to help.

 ## 6. Making the journey matter

Research an aid and development organisation that has a gift catalogue your family could use.

If you want to make a difference you can't just leave it for other people to do, you have to step up and accept the challenge. Just because a problem seems hopeless, it doesn't mean it's unsolvable. (Taylor, 10)

Consumer Advocacy

 ## 1. Where we're headed

To use our money and time to be more ethical and, where necessary, to get greedy companies to do the right thing!

 ## 2. Packing our bags: what we need to know, or something to stimulate our thinking

In the book *The Abundance of Less*, Marcy Pusey writes about her family's experiment to spend a year without buying anything new! They made exceptions for a few essential items and for artistic hand-made items. They saved money and saved waste, but they also discovered what they cared about and how easy it was to be happy with less. Happier even!

A friend who also did this exercise for a year said, 'It has been interesting to witness people's response to what I'm doing. From bewilderment, cynicism, and fear for the economy, to curiosity and wholehearted support. It also hasn't been enough. I'm acutely aware of how much more we could do to change [our] consumerism, waste, greed, ethical purchasing and ethical disposal of products.' What would your friends say about your lifestyle? What difference would it make if lots of people became more ethical with their purchasing power?

There are many reasons to try consuming less. Another way to look at it is to consume wisely. Most of the world's chocolate comes from West Africa. Our 'need' for this luxury has become so overwhelming that greedy organisations have ripped off and even enslaved farmers of cocoa beans. I don't want to eat chocolate that *children* have been forced to pick the cocoa beans for! I will only buy chocolate that has a 'Fair-Trade' sticker.

When many of us do this, and tell the companies, we are being advocates for the child workers. I also joined groups of people in advocacy campaigns to write letters to chocolate companies asking them to make sure they were being fair to farmers. When we did this, other chocolate companies were forced to make sure their trade was fair to farmers too! Perhaps you've noticed there are many more fair-trade alternatives in the supermarket aisles now?

3. Reading the map: instructions or preparation

Fashion is another huge global industry that sometimes mistreats workers so we can have cheap, fast fashion. When you pay only a dollar or two for a T-shirt, who do you think misses out? We can get companies to become fairer by only buying from ethical fashion brands, and telling them so. We can post on any company's Facebook page to tell them!

Take this quiz to find out whether your fashion purchases make you 'planet saviours' or 'planet vampires': https://www.fashionfootprint. org/.

You can get an idea which fashion brands are most ethical using this Australian report: https://baptistworldaid.org.au/resources/ethical-fashion-guide/.

4. On the road: our conversation

Companies pay great attention to who is buying from them and how and why not!

* Count up how many T-shirts you have in your household. Can you work out which ones are from companies that treat their workers fairly?
* How can you decide what is a *need* and what is a *want*?
* What questions could we ask about the ethics of companies before we spend on something new?
* Write a post on the social media page of a company you love, asking them about their ethical practices.

* Go to https://www.footprintcalculator.org/ to work out how many planets your family is using.

 ## 5. Unpacking

* How do you feel about your footprint scores? Who is missing out if you are using more than your fair share?
* How do you feel about your spending practices?
* Work out as a family what you might try to do differently.

 ## 6. Making the journey matter

We can also make sure our savings only support ethical investments.

We can get solar panels or ride our bikes more often to save energy.

We can ask our local butcher whether the animals they use are treated well.

What other ideas do you have?

Kids around the world need us to help make sure the planet is there for all to share!

Climate Justice

 ## 1. Where we're headed

To have a family conversation about climate change and its implications for others so our family can understand each other's views and work together towards a family response.

 ## 2. Packing our bags: what we need to know, or something to stimulate our thinking

When I went to Nepal, one reason it was so cold was that they had rolling electricity outages. Different areas were only allowed electricity eight hours at a time. Sometimes you got the middle-of-the-night eight-hour shift. This meant no hot water, businesses couldn't function – it seemed crazy! I discovered it was because of climate change. With such big mountains, hydro-electricity using the power of water raging downhill works well there. The monsoon – a season of big rains – powered the hydro. Climate change meant the monsoon season had shrunk from three months to two, so there was no longer enough water.

This was ten years ago. Now I've met people from Pacific Islands who have had rising oceans flood their schools and hospitals, and they are planning their moves. They will be 'climate refugees'. In Australia we've had devastating bushfires, and we're in danger of losing the Great Barrier Reef as the ocean heats up.

Climate change is increasing the number of natural disasters around the world and their severity. This impacts less-developed countries more, where people don't have the resources to cope and rebuild. Development organisations are now teaching people disaster management and readiness skills.

This makes climate change an issue of justice. Countries like Australia and America have much bigger carbon footprints per person than the countries like Nepal or Pacific Islands – yet they feel the least pain and poorer countries feel the most. It's not fair.

3. Reading the map: instructions or preparation

* Some people have strong opinions about climate change and others don't care. Why do you think it has become such a heated issue?
* Did you or do you know anyone who attended student climate strikes? Why or why not?
* Sometimes this issue differs around age – is this true in your family?
* It's worth remembering that sometimes fear turns into anger.

4. On the road: our conversation

Let each member of your family talk for at least one minute about climate change. No interrupting!

* How much do your future grandchildren matter to you when you think about climate change?
* If disrespecting women is sexist, and disrespecting age is ageist, is 'futurist' a thing?
* How much responsibility do we have to developing countries who are vulnerable to the effects of climate change?
* How much responsibility do we have to animals and plants that are being affected by our use of resources?
* How much should we cut our energy use?
* How much should we rely on scientists to invent something or politicians to do something to stop climate change?
* How can we encourage politicians to do something on a large scale?

5. Unpacking

* Was your conversation theoretical or did it get emotional for anyone?
* Why do you think some people are afraid?
* How does our fear change the way we approach this issue?
* How does selfishness affect this issue?

6. Making the journey matter

Did you know: Twenty-eight videogame companies have pledged to reduce their emissions and put 'green' elements like planting trees into their games?[120] This is a UN initiative, and they have 970 million players between them, so it is a great plan.

One family who tried out this conversation decided that their next car will be electric. I've already helped the planet with my book!

What research can you do? Have you watched David Attenborough's *A Life on Our Planet*?

Have you checked your carbon footprint at https://www.footprint-calculator.org/ ? It's life-changing!

Seeking Safety

1. Where we're headed

To practise our empathy and advocacy skills in the challenging area of people seeking asylum from war, poverty or oppression.

2. Packing our bags: what we need to know, or something to stimulate our thinking

When my children were very young, I worked hard to be a good mother, and much of this involved taking them to good playgrounds! Around this time, our government started a policy of locking up people seeking asylum (or safety, a right agreed upon by most countries in the United Nations). This included families with children. I didn't know much at the time, but all of my maternal instinct screamed at me that this was not right. Kids need to play! I joined a group called *ChilOut* (short for Children Out of Detention), and we marched and wrote and spoke up, and eventually, our government let all of the families out into the community as they waited for their applications to be processed.

Several years later, we took an asylum seeker into our home for a year as he waited, not allowed to work. We heard his story and saw his sadness. We ate his delicious cooking, and he encouraged my son to ask out a girl at church (at their wedding recently, they credited his matchmaking). This political issue is a real-life story for our family. He's now an official refugee, but he misses his own children dreadfully.

In our world today, 65.6 million people are refugees or displaced from their homes within their own country. More than half of these are children and teenagers under 18. For those of us living in peaceful democracies with enough money for our needs and our wants, this is hard to imagine. A new wave of 'climate refugees' is possible in the near future too. It's especially hard to imagine needing to flee from war. Watching so many movies with war as a backdrop doesn't always help us feel empathy. Sometimes, we can accidentally treat real-life refugees as extras in a movie instead.

3. Reading the map:
instructions or preparation

In 2017, World Vision Australia ran a campaign that was a little different from its annual 40-hour famine event (where people get sponsored to go without food for 40 hours in solidarity and to raise funds for people living in extreme poverty). They ran a backpack challenge where people were sponsored to live with only the essential items in their backpacks for 40 hours to raise awareness and money for refugee ration packs.

Every year, Act for Peace runs a 'Ration Challenge' in various countries where people eat the same food that a Syrian refugee is given by the UN for a week.[121] It's a tiny amount of very bland food. For example, under 2kg of rice, 400g flour, 170g lentils, 85g dried chickpeas, a small tin of sardines, a tin of kidney beans and 330ml vegetable oil … for a week.

This creates compassion and helps to raise money for *real* emergency ration packs. You can check it out here: https://www.rationchallenge.org/.

4. On the road:
our conversation

* Discuss **the idea of** eating refugee rations. **Could you try it?**
* Has anyone in your family met a refugee? My husband's father became a refugee at nine years old. Spend some time imagining what that might be like, or why it might be necessary.
* Imagine you had to pack a bag to flee tonight. What would you put in your backpack? What would you miss most about your home? Your country?

5. Unpacking

Hearing about terrible problems can be upsetting. The best way to manage our distress is to do something useful. Talking about it is useful as it builds understanding and empathy. How are you feeling now? When I ask my friend how I can help him, he always asks for prayer – for himself and for the family he can't care for himself.

 ## 6. Making the journey matter

Is there a movie or documentary in your area that you could watch to learn more about refugees? Read up at the UN Refugee Agency site: https://www.unhcr.org/en-au/.

What organisations do you know that support refugees in your area? How do they encourage people like your family to be involved?

Is there someone you know who you could invite over and ask about their life?

Thinking of three good things to be grateful for should be easy this week!

If I was in Charge...

 ## 1. Where we're headed

We will play a game that will help us think about privilege, rights and responsibilities. As a bonus, it will teach us philosophy and politics without even realising it! All this will make us better global citizens with empathy for people in other societies, and for the people who make up the rules!

 ## 2. Packing our bags: what we need to know, or something to stimulate our thinking

John Rawls was a philosopher who thought about justice in the world. He believed inequality through an accident of birth was not fair. He believed people should have freedom, but only if it didn't take away someone else's freedom to flourish.[122] And he thought we should show particular care for the least advantaged. So he designed a thought experiment called 'The Veil of Ignorance' to help people find fair principles of justice.

 ## 3. Reading the map: instructions or preparation

Imagine you are at the start of the world. Nature exists but people don't exist yet. They're coming soon though. Societies will exist too. You are about to choose how all people, including yourself, will live together when they arrive, but the catch is you will have a veil of ignorance!

This means that you don't know how you will live in this future. You don't know what gender you'll be or what 'country' you'll be born into. You don't know whether you'll have a loving family or be desperately poor. You could be intelligent or rich. But you might be sick and have to work very hard. You would be placed in one at random.

To make this feel more real, you could make some cards to draw out of a hat to decide who gets what.

* Country cards
* Gender cards
* Health cards
* Money cards

It will be fun imagining possible outcomes! (Don't choose just yet though.)

This, of course, means you can't just plan a society that will work for you. There's no point acting out of self-interest. The game begins as you decide what rules should govern how people live together. The trouble is, some rules will advantage some people and might disadvantage others ...

 # 4. On the road: our conversation

Some considerations as you start:

* Should people live in families or should teenagers live together?
* Should everyone get paid the same amount for hours worked?
* Should people pay tax?
* What might tax pay for?
* What happens if people hurt each other?
* What happens if people can't work?
* How should education work?

After you create your society, draw a card that tells you what gender you will be, what country you will be born into, and what your socio-economic status will be. Does the society you created work for you?

 # 5. Unpacking

* Are you aware you just became politicians?!
* Was it fun or difficult to make decisions for everybody?
* How does your world compare with the real world?
* What would you like to be different in the real world?

6. Making the journey matter

Watch for ways this game makes you think about the real world and fairness.

Visiting a Local Politician

 ## 1. Where we're headed

To turn some of our new skills and purpose into advocacy action by planning a visit to our local politician, showing that we care and asking for their help!

 ## 2. Packing our bags: what we need to know, or something to stimulate our thinking

Over several years I was a member of a group of 300 people who visited nearly all our national politicians in Parliament House to ask them to increase foreign aid to people living in extreme poverty. The politicians had agreed to this in principle by signing a United Nations pledge, but it wasn't happening in action. One year we asked to increase aid for 'WASH' – water and sanitation hygiene. With 50 percent of the hospital beds in very poor countries used for diarrhoea, helping villages build toilets is life-saving! Not sexy, so harder to fundraise for, but extremely effective and a good use of government aid.

We did our research and worked out just where and how much would be most helpful. We made information sheets to give to the politicians with exactly what we were asking for. We built a huge model toilet and used it for photo opportunities. We had all ages with us, and the kids gave politicians a roll of toilet paper and a bar of soap to remind them of our visit.

I started doing these annual visits for work, but soon took my sons along. The thrill of using our democratic power for a cause we care about was worth sharing! They loved it. It was hard and a bit scary, but it made a difference. Now, post-COVID-19, we are waiting to find out how small villages have coped without good WASH. I like to think some people have coped better, though, because of our previous advocacy and aid.

I just asked my son what he'd tell you about his experience visiting parliament. He said it was 'definitely intimidating, but also cool – it was the most influential thing a person can do!' If you think about it, it's very strategic – we can make a much bigger impact if we can get new laws or big changes that make a difference for lots of people at once.

3. Reading the map: instructions or preparation

The key to success for these visits was good preparation. Researching what we care about and what will help most makes a politician's job much easier. They care when they know we care. They are there to represent our concerns. And politicians love a visit from kids!

What organisations are working in the area you care about? They might have useful information, statistics or solutions you could bring to your politician's attention.

Find out the name of your local politician. We have state senators and local representatives in Australia, and they have local offices we can visit. Who represents your interests to the government? Find out their phone number and email address – they will have a website. Find out what they care about too – maybe it's the same as you, hurray – or maybe you can recognise their conflicting pressures too.

Who else might like to help you or visit with you? Do you know an expert in the area you care about?

Make an appointment saying what topic your visit might be about. When you visit, be polite and respectful. They have a hard job and saying 'thank you' can make a big difference!

4. On the road: our conversation

Discuss as a family what you might want to talk to your politician about. What research do you need to do?

Imagine you're preparing for a debate. What questions might your politician have that you could prepare to answer? What aspect of your issue might each of you talk about? (Everyone should have a go at talking – age is no barrier!)

Talk together about:

* Why you care about this
* What personal experience you have with this problem
* Stories you can tell about it
* The arguments that will be the most persuasive
* What exactly you would like them to do for you

 # 5. Unpacking

* How did it go? Did it feel exciting or scary? Do you feel optimistic or cynical?
* Could you tell your school magazine or local newspaper what you plan to do?
* Could you write an article describing your thoughts before and after your visit?

 # 6. Making the journey matter

Go and visit your politician! Take a friend. Make them a card or a poster. Have fun – be as creative as you can – it will be more memorable.

Visit https://www.unicef.org/child-rights-convention to learn about *The Convention on the Rights of the Child*. This might help you in future research.

You could research Malala Yousafzai – the youngest-ever Nobel Prize winner. She's inspiring in her advocacy for education for girls!

Watch UNICEF Goodwill Ambassador Millie Bobby Brown talk to three inspiring young activists from around the world. They tell their stories here: https://www.youtube.com/watch?v=0DDYLjEC4cw.

They are discussing how they have helped out with bullying, education and the pandemic.

Our Family Mission

 ## 1. Where we're headed

To create a sense of purpose as a family – to plan how we'd like to contribute to the world!

 ## 2. Packing our bags: what we need to know, or something to stimulate our thinking

Some families figure out what's important to them and the way they want to make a difference. Then they put their time, energy and resources like money towards this mission. This might look like:

* leaving home to live in another country in order to help people there
* supporting their local soccer club by playing and volunteering
* joining a church and commit to helping the people there through life
* volunteering in nature
* giving financial help to extended family or to helping organisations
* cook for people or have people in need come to stay.

How would you like to live as a family?

We know from research that people who have meaning and purpose are happier. It makes sense that this might make us happier as a family too.

For inspiration, visit https://howrichami.givingwhatwecan.org/how-rich-am-i to get an idea of where you stand in the world and what your generosity could do. It will literally tell you how many lives you could save!

3. Reading the map: instructions or preparation

A mission statement should be a short, exciting explanation saying whom you'd like to serve and how.

Here's an example of two charities' mission statements:

* Watts of Love is a global solar lighting nonprofit bringing people the power to raise themselves out of the darkness of poverty.
* First Descents provides life-changing outdoor adventures for young adults (age 18-39) impacted by cancer.

A more personal one might be:

* To positively impact the life of every person I meet.

Author Andy Andrews helped his family craft a mission statement by asking these questions:

* What is important?
* Where do we want to go?
* What does 'the best' look like for us?
* How do we want to act?
* What is the legacy we want to leave behind?

Here's what they came up with:

> 'In the Andrews family, our mission is to arise each day with grateful hearts and smiling faces, determined to glorify, serve and trust in God. We live by the highest standards of moral character and integrity. We love, respect, encourage and defend each other. And we're noble stewards of the resources entrusted to us.'[123]

4. On the road: our conversation

Make sure everyone in your family has a piece of paper and a pen (coloured is more creative but whatever ...).

Ask each person to answer these questions – with a word, a story, a picture, anything!

1. What things do you like doing together as a family?

2. What do you like most about being in this family?
3. What would you love to do more of as a family?
4. How does this family help you get through life?
5. How does this family help other people – friends, family, charities?
6. Do you know any ways other families help?
7. What would you like to see get better in the world?
8. How could your family help make this happen?

Try to write a personal mission statement from these ideas:

'With my life, I would like to ...' or

'Our family cares about ...'.

5. Unpacking

Get a bigger piece of paper to record the ideas that everyone in the family agrees with. As you go through each question, ask each family member to share their ideas, then record the ones other family members are keen to agree with.

Try to turn this group of ideas into one or two sentences that everyone is happy not only to agree with, but to enthusiastically sign up their lives to!

6. Making the journey matter

You could make a poster of this one for your home too! The real test, though, will be finding ways to put it into practise.

Part III

Unpacking

the Adventure

Congratulations! You're a family who cares! Now that you know how it works, it's your turn!

Take turns inventing your next family conversations! Perhaps one of you is passionate about plastics in the ocean or not eating meat? Maybe you recently learnt about an ethical dilemma or you've learnt a new thing at work or school you'd like to share?

Now that you're experts, you might find these structured conversations are a great way to manage 'no-go' topics. Let your kids ask you any question. Is this the time to air any family skeletons in the closet?!

Here's the template to copy and keep the conversations going! Just do a little research and think up some questions. Enjoy!

You can download a printable version at

www.raisingkidswhocare.info

(Conversation Title)

1. Where we're headed

----

2. Packing our bags:
   what we need to know, or
   something to stimulate our
   thinking

----

3. Reading the map: instructions or preparation

---

4. On the road: our conversation

---

5. Unpacking

----

6. Making the journey matter

Conclusion:

Making the Journey Matter

Thanks for joining me on this trip to make the world a more caring place. I hope your family has enjoyed it and been enriched by your conversations. I trust you've built a good foundation for future communication. In summary, and because none of us are perfect, let me leave you with three tips:

Communication is everything.

Focus first on building a culture of good communication in your family. After all, we don't know what struggles are around the corner, but we know we're going to need good communication skills to get through them together. It's also the only real tool we need for conflict resolution. If you'd like, you could even take a communication course or visit a counsellor together. Above all, learn to listen. Seek first to understand, then to be understood. Good communication uses manners and respect to show kindness. What's more, if we treat our kids with respect, they'll refuse to be disrespected by others.

Expect more.

Kids are amazing. They're always our little babies (my mum still talks about when I was a baby!), so as parents, we're always a developmental stage or two behind what they're really up to. They're learning abstract thinking and concrete knowledge in school that surpasses what we remember. What's more, they'll rise to the level of our expectations of them. Kids around the world are leading their communities – let's prepare ours to change their worlds!

Always be watching for ways you can encourage them to <u>respond</u> to issues they see in the world.

'Don't ask kids what they want to be when they grow up, but what problems they want to solve. This changes the conversation from who do I want to work for, to what do I need to learn to be able to do that.' Jaime Casap

Actions speak loudest.

Role modelling is the most powerful thing you'll ever do as a parent. Our kids copy us – from our gestures to our values – so we need to work on ourselves first. They also learn more experientially than from any book or lecture.

- Take them out with you into the world. Apprentice them and learn with them.
- Volunteer together.
- Write to, visit or cook for sick or elderly friends as a family together.
- Consider an overseas volunteering trip rather than a resort holiday.
- Participate in something big together – most organisations have fundraising events.
- Talk about what you believe and how you demonstrate that.
- Talk about the world as you're living it.
- Just be authentic and inclusive. Do things to show you care, and you'll raise kids who care too.

But also: don't be too hard on yourself! I am certainly my own worst critic, and it took a long time to realise that love covers a multitude of ineptitude. It's never too late to improve your communication, resolve a conflict or even change your family culture. Just jump in somewhere and enjoy the journey!

A story ...

An elderly wise man was educating his young students about life.

He told them, 'A battle is going on within me. It is a dreadful battle and it is between two great lions. One lion is wicked: he is fear, rage, jealousy, sadness, greed, pride, self-pity, shame, hatred, weakness, lies, rivalry and superiority.

'The other lion is good: he is happiness, harmony, love, trust, sharing, peace, modesty, gentleness, compassion, friendship, understanding, charity, truth, kindness and loyalty.

'This same battle is going on inside you and inside every other person as well.'

They considered his words for a while, then one of the students asked his teacher, 'Which lion will win?'

The old sage replied thoughtfully, 'The one you feed the most.'

(Author unknown)

I've just started reading *Humankind: A Hopeful History* by Rutger Bregman, and he quotes this same story, only it's a wolf not a lion.[124] The premise of his book is a radical idea confirmed by science and lived experience, but ignored by rulers, the news and history books: it's that people are basically decent. He suggests we imagine a plane crash where the cabin is filling with smoke – what will happen? Will people panic and trample each other to get out, or will they help each other, heroically saving strangers on the way? Most people say chaos, but most act caringly. And the more we notice the care, the more caring we will expect and become.

Many stories share a common plot structure: a hero faces a challenge – perhaps between good and evil – with a guide to help them overcome their challenges. Think Frodo in Lord of the Rings: to save the world, he had to get rid of the ring that brewed selfishness and greed in anyone who held it, with Gandalf guiding him. I hope I have been a useful guide as you journeyed through the wide range of activities in this book.

I think we all have the potential for good and evil within us. Life consists of battles against the fear, rage, jealousy and so on in each of us, and against the same in others as we bump up against their battles. Yet when we're young, Disney movies paint the 'baddie' in black and the 'goodie' in white. Then as we get older, we realise that life is much more complicated than that, and that we aren't so different. Recognising that everyone is battling the same things helps us have compassion and grace for others doing it tough.

And really that is where change starts: compassion and grace. By developing those traits, we can make positive changes. It would be great to change the world, but really, few of us will make history. The trick is for each of us to improve a little bit. Our small acts of friendship or courage, of generosity or compassion, knit together to shape history. Every time one of us stands up for our beliefs or for someone else, we create more of the grand tapestry of life. Millions of little stitches, all different, but all inspiring and life changing. Keep knitting until that tapestry covers up any dirty marks of poverty or injustice or hopelessness. That's how to weave a meaningful life.

I know my boys are a testament to what intentionality combined with love can do for our parenting. I hope this book has been a testament to my belief that the best way to live is for us together – caring for each other. My belief that some stuff matters more. My belief that kids need us to inspire them to care, even when we know this might sometimes be the harder way to live. Most of my beliefs come from the words and actions of Jesus and I hope I have also been encouraging that he is worth a look too.

Bless you and your family as you grapple with how to feed your good lions. The world needs families like you. Bless your commitment to growing your hearts, minds and characters, to better contribute to the world and its people. It's my prayer that your family is strengthened through this book. And that you each find your unique opportunities to spread happiness and harmony around you as a result.

Spread the love with other families in 'The Justice Games'

If you've enjoyed these conversations, perhaps you could invite friends or other families to join you. Even better, explore my next project 'The Justice Games' which has experiential games to help you explore issues as well as guided conversations. The 'simulation' games help you experience an issue, and they need more people, so the idea is to get a group of families playing together. Our website www.thejusticegames.org will tell you where to find an event near you, or you could run one yourself.

Get peer group pressure working for you! You could put on an event at your school, church or sports club to get other families sharing their conversations. While you could use the conversations in this book, I've created 'The Justice Games' to include group games and activities as well as conversations. The events will stimulate your family conversations in a wider group. They are 'meaningful fun'.

Each event will have a theme around an issue: one on consumerism, one on conflict resolution, one on technology, one on money, another on resilience. It might be easier to get your family talking when others are doing it at the same time and sharing their thoughts. A bit of competition gets everyone excited. Throw in a meal at the end, and you'll have a great family night out.

Please stay in touch – it's likely that your experiences will help other families too.

You can share your thoughts with me via email to

susy@raisingkidswhocare.info

or find out more through

communications@thejusticegames.org.

THANKS FOR READING MY BOOK!

The world looks forward to the caring contributions your family will make as a result!

If you'd like to download a printable template for taking notes during your conversations,

and

If you'd like to be kept in the loop when I can't help writing new conversations about current or important issues with new information,

then... you can!

Just visit: www.raisingkidswhocare.info

I hope you've found this book helpful, and I'd absolutely love to hear your thoughts. Writing is lonely and I'd love to know it's been worthwhile!

So please could you leave me your honest review of the book on the book's Amazon page?

Reviews are crucial to get the word out to others who might find this book helpful too.

Appendix 1:

More Parent Survey Responses

1. In what ways does your child amaze you or give you joy?

- Our sons are a constant joy. One example was when our older son put on a magic show at a homeless shelter. I could tell he was afraid, but he went through with it anyway!
- It brings me joy when my sons show kindness and thoughtfulness to others without encouragement and where it has involved sacrifice on their part / putting the needs of others before their own.
- Today my daughter bought me flowers just because she loves me xx tears of joy xx
- When my son was asked to go and find his shoes and put them on, his younger sister (only 1 year old) rushed off to find them and give them to him. Beautiful helper.
- Child 2 standing up to people bullying her friends despite being scared.
- When we watched news about refugees and he showed such empathy with them

2. Which of these issues are you concerned about for your child?

Lack of Community Support and Isolation

- We are all so busy with our own concerns that we often don't consider reaching out to others outside our immediate circle
- Few activities available for older teens outside of sports.

- General public don't seem to embrace children and the energetic chaos they bring

Peer Group Pressure
- A normal part of growing up but the "bad stuff" seems so much worse than 20-30 years ago
- It's different for each. Not worried about it for #1... more so for #2...
- Things are not always as they seem and no matter how much you think your child will resist peer pressure the wrong person can make a huge impact.
- I did worry a lot about peer pressure and if they would be tempted to do things they shouldn't although fortunately they were so busy with sports that they never had time for anything much other than training.

Anxiety and Depression
- Child 1 has a history of anxiety - finds it difficult to make a decision for herself
- Because I have struggled myself, I fear my kids may have inherited it.
- Child 2 is a born worrier - we work hard on helping her to relax, considering if the issue is a legitimate worry, and working on being brave!! Hard work, but we're getting there.
- The incidence among boys and young men is very high and my son is stubborn and sometimes quite focused on Sci - fi, I wonder about his ability to cope with reality.
- Youngest son suffered from this as a young teen - spent many months sleeping during the day and being up all night.

Consumerism
- We are our own worst enemies in this department... we have the means to want to "give" to our children but the lesson we often teach despite our good intentions is about the "get"

- Neither child has an income, so tends to have a limited view of the responsibility of money
- Takes after their mother :)
- Very hard not to be influenced as consumerism permeates the world they live in.
- Child 1 is anti-consumerist and he greatly influences the other 3
- They think if something breaks you just buy a new one to replace it. This can amount to lack of respect for their belongings (and others)
- The "need" to have more stuff, new stuff all the time - that attitude worries me.
- It's so pervasive. "How to avoid consumerism without feeling like you are a teenage outcast?"

Technology

- A constant battle as a parent to encourage a healthy balance. Boys in particular seem more obsessive in this department (a gross generalisation I know :)
- Even at 6 months she is drawn to screens (which isn't great for her developing brain). With the amount around us in our day to day lives - it's hard to escape!
- I love technology and see that technology has many good points. At the same time, I work in ministry and see the effect that the overuse of technology and over-reliance on technology has on the development of children. All things in moderation is my consideration with technology - boundaries are a must if we want to parent healthy and respectful children.
- I already notice my children's tendency to imitate the shows they watch on tv and worry that they could be exposed to something inappropriate at friend's houses etc.
- Not worried but cautious and mindful
- Technology has made children less innocent.

Early sexualisation and pornography

- Unavoidable exposure to media images unless you live in a cave. I would like to think that I will be able to encourage (?enforce) good choices in the clothing department as we venture further into this territory
- We live in a virtually advertising-free household, which reduces (but doesn't eliminate) their exposure to unhelpful messages
- It's just a reality in modern culture
- What my girls will be exposed to is likely to be so different to what I was exposed to
- I am terrified about pornography and unsure exactly how we best address that
- Maybe it's a girl thing or because of her personality, but she's 6 and already makes comments related to body image and is very particular about clothes etc.
- The younger 3 searched up some stuff - it was horrible! We talked to them about how upset we were and that the problem with porn is that it is fake and destroys relationships
- My younger two sons both found ways to access porn.

Communication Skills
- Soooo important for them to be able to talk about "stuff". I have learnt to recognise that bad / unusual behaviour might be them communicating that something is wrong and giving them the space and opportunity to turn that into words
- Despite our best efforts you can't change someone. We can only continue to correct and advise.

Self-centredness
- A normal childhood trait to some extent but perhaps we are inadvertently contributing to this by allowing the "I want" mentality to be normal / ok (refer to consumerism comments)
- It's a part of them growing up. I hate the self-centred stuff, but I do recognise there is an element where they are differentiating

- Goes hand in hand with consumerism... we live in a world that is all about me.

3. **Does your family have specific ways to deal with any of these issues?**

- Talking through things - sometimes it takes patience - waiting til they are ready to talk.
- We try to show different points of view, we point out what the effects of consumerism, peer pressure and try to balance all activities, also that they can control their emotions and not to pre-empt outcomes before they occur.
- We have tended to encourage the kids to take on age-appropriate responsibilities. This has fostered a degree of self-sufficiency which I think contributes to self-confidence and thinking beyond the "I".
- My wife and I try to lead by example in the way that we live.
- Being part of a church community with a thriving youth group and positive young people with strong morals and faith, makes me confident that my daughters will have a peer group and positive role models surrounding them in their formative years, even if there are many negative influences in society.
- Spending lots of time. Giving real answers about things and being honest about sad or difficult things.
- My view is that the healthiest children are those willing to "fail". Fear of failure is a very debilitating characteristic and appears to be more problematic in girls due to their greater self-awareness. I give my children permission to fail in anything they're trying in. My son is good with it, my daughter won't try anything that risks failure. She is aware that she is that way but can't change it. Most of her female friends are the same. We all need to be able to laugh at ourselves and not be so self-conscious.
- Intentionally being available, creating conversation when we can. Sharing values with our community and encouraging trusted relationships with others. Seeking

support when I'm unsure what to do or feel ignorant about an issue.

- Quite frankly, and don't spread it around, we've always relied on cultivating a snobbish approach - well of course other people do those things but we're not like that, we know better; also, a sense of noblesse oblige on account of one's own education and opportunities. It sounds awful when you spell it out, but it seems to have worked a treat with regards to body piercing, binge drinking, skipping school, having an informed perspective on politics, considering oneself powerless or entitled to special treatment or handouts, claiming special consideration for exams, not taking responsibility and so forth. I would recommend it. Can be used at any income level in any suburb.

- Being intentional and proactive in dealing with these issues is vital. Have dealt with exposure to porn already with our oldest which highlighted the need to be super vigilant when it comes to technology use - as we had been quite careful with how/when the internet was accessed but that wasn't enough. Also realised the need to talk about the dangers of porn with kids earlier rather than later - we didn't expect to be dealing with it in primary school!

- At this young age in my children, we tend to focus on building acceptance and confidence in communication, understanding emotions and supporting them to learn how to manage these. We also try to support their understanding of the needs of others where opportunities arise in their everyday lives. We have an intention of always being honest with our children, which means answering questions with truth, explaining the truth behind our decisions and things that impact on them etc. My greatest challenge is probably managing my own reactions and emotions to their behaviours amidst my own needs - saying sorry to them when I have stuffed up is helpful for this!

- We try to build confidence through encouragement and independence. And when things don't work out, then we dust ourselves off and try again if possible. We don't give up.

- Professional help needed after non-acceptance of parental reassurance to deal with depression, anxiety & self-esteem difficulties.
- Re self-centredness & consumerism I talk to them regularly about how rich we are and how much less other people have. We try to discuss social issues when they come up in the news etc. Also re consumerism I have a rule about gifts being just for birthdays & Christmas, any other "wants" must be earned by doing odd jobs and using their own pocket money.
- If ever these issues exist, we make sure that we talk to our children to discuss, clarify and find solutions.
- Speak about them out loud. Don't presume they don't have experience with these issues.
- We talk a lot about their feelings, if they don't like a situation to speak up and tell someone. If they feel something is wrong then it probably is, go with your instincts.
- We limit screen time and extra-curricular activities. Try to stick to good food and rest. Get places on time. Play in the mud a lot. That all helps...
- Bedtime prayer and talking helps with problems or issues. Dinner time question jar is good for conversation and insight.
- We introduce early discipline, time limit for play with gadgets, say sorry, please and forgiving others - along with clear explanation for her age.
- We basically just try to reinforce her self-confidence and empowerment. We try to ensure she's never scared at home and that she's completely loved and free to talk to us about anything. We listen to her and take her seriously and try to set a good example.
- Open communication and talking about everything. I also have a great relationship with my sister who I can lean on for external help if needed. She has done many years of therapy (on herself) so she is very self-aware

and helpful with sticky situations. I would always go to external professional help if needed.

- We've always offered lots of opportunities for the kids to make choices & experience the consequences, good & bad. We've role modelled volunteering, thinking of others, choosing to reduce our consumerism by having secondhand clothes/op shopping/recycling etc
- I tend to Google when I get to each stage of their lives, so I know what I'm up for and best practice out there. I also read articles from social media on giving your children confidence, etc. We are so lucky to have so much information available to us.
- We have been greatly helped by Danny Silks, "Loving Your Kids on Purpose" series.
- We are very close and do a lot of things together. We work hard to build up our children to believe in themselves and their abilities. When my son is anxious, we allow him alone time if that is what he wants but are always around if he needs us. Sometimes a walk and chat with one of us is all he needs. Going to the gym with his sister or a bike ride with his Dad can bring him out of it. He and I bake together and chat together. He just needs to know that he is not alone and can share his worries with people who love him unconditionally.
- We limit our boys on their use of technology at home and monitor closely what they watch
- We have always talked a lot as a family, either all together or individually when things concerned us, and we continue to talk a lot, so if the boys have problems, they're happy to come to us.

4. **What's one opportunity or event that has helped your child grow as a person?**

- We distributed Christmas Hampers to nursing home residents as a family on Christmas Day. The kids still talk about it as their best Christmas ever.
- Travelling to Manila and being friends with people living in poverty.

- Our younger son has grown as a person since we started sponsoring a child overseas.
- Having the opportunity to help others has taken their thoughts off themselves
- Having a little sister to look after, look out for, and share with.
- Changing school. Being accepted for who he is and his qualities by another group of people.
- The relationship with his grandmother makes him aware of how important he is in someone's life and the responsibility this brings (all positive).
- Travelling overseas without us.
- Going on a camp with other young people
- My son took a toy from a neighbour's house. When I found it and asked him where he got it - I made him go the house to return the item and apologise.
- Coming to church... They participate in the 5pm congregation with young adults and youth. And they really take them under their wing, gives him role models to look up to...
- Doing "Live Below the Line" (Act for Peace) as a family
- Involving them in ministry opportunities we have as a family - running a yearly youth camp and engaging in a short-term opportunity in China have probably been the standouts.
- Visiting Vanuatu where the people were happy but had little material possessions.
- When she sees other children upset it forces her to think about their feelings. This inevitably makes her more compassionate towards other kids
- My oldest son works for a private school as a coach. he saw what was happening to the kids that were not making the grade. Remembering how he felt - he took the opportunity to write an email to every coach and teacher, reminding them of the sensitivities of such acts, and to consider the boys feelings, and perhaps humiliation when telling their parents they didn't make the grade. He posted various situations and solutions to

them. The response he received was amazing and the principal of this prestigious school welcomed such advice and heeded everyone to take note.

- Child 1 took part in a Model United Nations Assembly representing Bangladesh. This gave her a great understanding of how the UN operates and ignited more interested in pursuing something in this area of study. Also, her leadership role in the student-led trip to India helped build on her leadership skills and increased her confidence.

- Being humiliated by others "judging" her. She now knows to choose her friends carefully. Having selfish people stay with us for weeks has also been helpful in character training - "do you want to be like that when you grow up"?

- Getting involved in volunteer activities: Clean up Australia, packing Christmas hampers, food drives and helping out friends when they need it. Has given them the sense that they can make a difference in the world.

- Raising money for TEAR Australia, to give to poor people overseas.

- Adversity- my son has been crying on the playground with no friends to play with. A new kid arrived at his school this week and he's taken him under his wing. I like that he's taken this opportunity to look out for another kid in a similar situation of not having friends/ connections and reaching out to him.

- She's spent a lot of time in hospital so that's hugely influenced her courage and her caring about other people. She's enormously sensitive to anyone who is hurt, sick or upset and wants to comfort them and make them better.

5. Sample Parents' Mission Statements

- To encourage our children to become kind and decent adults who have purpose in their lives.

- To guide them and give them skills to help them though life. To treat other as they'd like to be treated, and be grateful for what you have, not look to others for your happiness.

- To love, listen and encourage children through their life journey that puts others before themselves.
- To nurture and support my child with the unconditional love that allows him to choose a life journey that gradually leads to his best potential.
- To assist my children to become compassionate and well-rounded individuals who have the tools to cope with any adversity thrown their way, so they come out ok!
- To raise happy and healthy boys that are comfortable in their own skin and are always kind to those that deserve kindness.
- To raise healthy and happy children who contribute to a just, constructive and peaceful society
- To provide an environment where my child feels safe, loved and supported; has opportunities and is supported to learn and develop (including emotionally, spiritually, etc); learns about the world and how she fits into it; and ultimately learns what life is really about which leads to her own personal relationship with Jesus
- To help my children develop faith, skills and independence in a supportive environment so that they can contribute to others in the world around them for years to come.
- Keep an open mind, grow with your child and make the most of the journey.
- To help my family work as a team, help each other reach our different potentials, and to love each other and others more each day.
- To raise loving content children who help make a positive difference in the world
- To help my child develop critical thinking skills, navigate the grey areas of life and ultimately approach problems with and open mind and a sense of self reliance

- Share wisdom. Reduce instruction. Encourage action.
- Love, empower, encourage, mentor, have fun.
- To show through my own actions that life is not too serious. Work hard, care about others and achieve everything you need in life to be happy above all else.
- To grow myself out of a job
- Things always look much better in the morning
- Be kind and patient, be loving and fair, keep your ears and eyes open, always be present, always forgive your child and always forgive yourself.
- To give them the skills they need to be a valuable contributor to society and to find inner contentment.
- Don't sacrifice the relationship for the rules
- To raise a child who passionately loves God and sacrificially loves others.
- To love unconditionally, to always listen, to talk to and not 'at' and to always be there no matter what.
- Provide a strong secure loving family base for them to step out from. Provide a clear set of values and worldview. Facilitate hope and enthusiasm and a can do/why not attitude.
- To let your kids to create their own mission and be smart enough to know when to support, encourage, shut up, and get out of the way!

Anything to Add?
- Health + activity + fitness + nutrition
- Life is about BALANCE
- I wish I wasn't so obsessed with homework and I wish I could be more 'in the moment' with them.
- I would like to see bullying addressed more in schools, from very early on such as kindergarten right through each school year
- Please read the book Knowing Me Knowing Them - Aha! Anyone writing a book about parenting will benefit greatly from this. Good luck! http://knowingme-knowingthem.com/

- I regret not making them meet and greet people properly when they were very young. They were shy so I let them hide behind me and didn't force them to say hello properly. If I had my time over again, I would be firmer as I think it would have taught them there was nothing to be afraid of, and that learning proper manners is actually quite liberating and takes anxiety away from social situations.
- Parenting is the hardest thing ever but the most satisfying & meaningful thing you can ever do. Don't try to be your child's friend, they need boundaries & within that you can be great buddies. Us mums are so hard on ourselves. We need to seek help & support & not be ashamed about it.
- Too often I see parents (myself included) resort to outbursts of anger, or giving in, or bribery etc because they've tried various strategies but are not getting the results that you're supposed to get. Also, if it takes a village to raise a child, our "villages" are often not helping, or not able to help. Parenting is often quite isolated, and people don't want to interfere with other people's parenting.
- I wish I was less selfish & busy, but my wife is awesome & makes up for it.
- The exam system is flawed and has created so many unnecessary pressures amongst young people.
- I wish more parents put manners, love, selflessness and generosity of spirit as high priorities rather than academic success and personal happiness.
- I wish we could all live more simply.
- I am so proud of my beautiful children and the amazing young adults they have become xx
- Parenting has been the greatest joy and simultaneously the greatest challenge of my life.
- Praying is the most important job as a parent.
- Based on our experience with our eldest I often wonder if we should have intervened more when she was in her later teens.

- Hard to be single parent with sole financial, emotional & practical responsibility for a child
- I wish we as individuals and as a couple were more equipped to deal with stress and conflict. We're learning to do this in counseling.
- The days are long and it's often tempting to just take the easy route- put the kids in front of the tv without checking what's on, or to ignore behaviour rather than correcting it. Day by day I need to remember the joy and privilege and responsibility of shaping these little people's lives.
- It's all in the past for me now and I wish I had been a better person myself at the time. It amazes me how well all the children have turned out.
- Talk with your children, don't shout at them. Think about how it feels if someone has ever shouted at you. fighting is for enemies. Thank you for listening to my perspective. Good luck with your book. X

APPENDIX 2:

MORE YOUNG ADULT SURVEY RESPONSES

1. **Can you give an example of when your parent(s) amazed you or brought you great joy? (grab the tissues)**

   - They once found a small bag containing more than $500 lying on the ground in cash, in a department store. Instead of taking it without anybody else's notice, they handed it in to the front desk. After it while, it was claimed by old lady astounded at their honesty but overjoyed with gratitude.

   - My mother amazes me and brings me great joy every single day :) :) Amazed: the times they let complete strangers stay with us, including a homeless man and an asylum seeker. Great joy: hysterics over family dinners, especially on holidays.

   - When I had leukaemia when I was 6 years old, and my parents made my welfare their main priority, putting their own needs and their needs as a married couple aside to care for me, support me and love me.

   - My parents bring me great joy when they are happy, it is a pure pleasure to watch.

   - My father once disclosed to me some of his personal struggles with depression as I was going through it myself, I had never known and it was probably the first real conversation we've had together.

   - I can think of a number of examples, but a few certainly "stick out" in my memory. One was when I had spent some time with my Dad, and we ended up going into a long, deep conversation on the car trip home. I distinctively remember my Dad telling me, "I love you, and I would die for you if I had to." I think that is one of the most powerful things someone has ever said to me. Other times include when my parents were willing to support me in some of my "lowest" times. I have struggled with mental health issues in the past, and my parents have always been there to listen (even though they may not fully understand), support me, and spend time with me. It's in those moments that they have amazed me, and (paradoxically) brought me great joy.

- During the 2003 bushfires my family lived in Duffy. We were stuck in the car while a fireball rolled past us and were surrounded by fire. Now an adult my parents have told me that they were so scared and had said their goodbyes to one another. Yet us kids had no idea, we just had hope that our parents would get us out. They didn't want us to worry. They are in my eyes, incredible.

- When my mum gave me at my 21st a necklace that had been bought for me by my dad (who had died when I was 2)

- Amaze me with how much hard work they do, how much they juggle, how they choose a job they love and are passionate about and how through all that they still have time to love, care and be present with me.

- I was amazed by the grace my Dad showed me when I crashed his car when I was 17.

- When they continually teach me to value preserving this earth we are on. Whether it be by excessively recycling, valuing other peoples discarded material possessions or in the way they tell me "Put more clothes on!" when I complain about being cold in our non-heated house. I just love the way I've been brought up to have an ethical/environmental conscious.

2. Did any of these issues affect you as a child?

Peer group pressure: *I did a lot of things that I don't agree with now because of pressure from peers. My best friend through a lot of school was also in retrospect quite manipulative in her* *agenda in our friendship.*

Consumerism: *Probably my earlier teenage years I was more interested in saving up for expensive clothes etc... There wasn't a single thing that changed that but gradually over time I became far less interested. Probably because of the kind of justice-focused/minimalistic Christian leaders I had and an increasing interest in secondhand goods...*

Technology: *technology can be distracting and also a social pressure to keep up with trends.*

Early sexualisation: *Nothing until high school thankfully, but high school makes you 'grow up' real quick in that regard because of everything that everyone else has seen/knows about and shares.*

Communication skills: *I found it difficult to open up to people about things that were really personal to me, because I feared shame, vulnerability and rejection.*

Not so much with me but my mother is a really bad communicator which caused a lot of family issues.

Self-confidence: *I've always had very poor self-confidence, but my parents (mum especially) have always believed in me and helped to give me confidence.*

3. **Did your parents have any specific ways to deal with any of these issues?**

Lack of community support: *church and living with extended family.*

Peer group pressure: *Let us use them as scapegoats if we ever didn't want to do something. Also we found our worth and identity in our family, community and faith, not just our friends/peers.*

Anxiety/depression: *Checked we were ok regularly. They moved my school at my request. When depressed they made sure I found a good psychologist.*

Consumerism: *Demonstrated generosity. Built a culture in our household of anti-consumerism. Technology: [robot voice]: 'get off now. you have been on the computer for 23hrs, 37mins and 42seconds.'*

Early sexualisation/pornography: *My parents were able to make us feel like we could talk about anything with them. I always thought that was quite extraordinary, and it helped me immensely in this area.*

Communication skills: *Mum and Dad worked really hard to get us to communicate our feelings. They were good examples in how they communicated with each other and put in the extra time/effort to try to get us to communicate how we were feeling. They also taught us the importance of open-ended questions.*

Self-centredness: *They put effort into trying to show us how we fit into the wider world. This included a trip to Vietnam and lots of lessons about the poor.*

Poor self-confidence, belief in their ability to effect change: *They have always been good at trying to see it from my point of view and respecting that I can make the right decision for myself*

- My parents have always encouraged conversation about those topics, especially at the dinner table, so that my brother and I didn't feel ashamed to bring those things up. (There were some issues that they talked to us about privately, as it wouldn't have been appropriately for the other sibling to hear). My parents have always encouraged my brother and I to share our opinion and our thoughts before they answered our questions or told us their opinion.

- My mum was always super open and honest, we had a close relationship and she always treated me like an adult which helped me in being able to talk to her about my issues openly and honestly. This always meant that I was never sheltered away from these real life issues and could attempt to deal with them like a mature adult.

- They led a lot by example and encouraged us to be more selfless doing things for others as a family. They also had open discussions about how we should love others.

- Being strict when they had to about what we could access and have, and consistently answering our questions of "Why?" with wisdom. Also having strong and long-term family friends who are invested in our lives, just as we are in theirs helped.

- My parents certainly weren't perfect. I often at times felt misunderstood and that I didn't "measure up". But they always reiterated to me that they loved me and were willing to do whatever it took to support me. Over time, they became better at communicating this. I think "unconditional positive regard" is so important in parenting - that no matter what, your parents are there for you, love you, and will support you regardless of what you "do" or "become".

- They wouldn't feed into my consumerist nature and limited the stuff they bought me which meant I had to work for it. Mum would also always chat to me about the big issues giving me gentle reminders. They were good at closely managing technology time, not so good at managing communication between family members.

- Loving and caring for me first. And trusting me, even when I went a bit wild. Because they trusted me I always told them to truth about where I was on the weekends and never lied like the other teens.

- They were never, never judgmental and I rarely got in trouble and have never been grounded. This lack of anger and punishment from my parents meant I wanted to be a better person and that our relationship was never tense because we didn't drive each other away. Because I knew home was always a safe place to go back to, I felt I could explore the world and find who I was. In the end I came out of this wild phase quickly because I had a taste of it and then didn't want it anymore. I think because I always open to explore what I needed to and find out for myself. And now my relationship with my parents is so close and strong.

- My parents' interactions with each other influenced me; they always expressed the importance of listening to what others have to say, giving them time and giving thoughtful consideration to any response.

4. **What's one event that helped you grow as a person?**

- Going to India with a student led month long expedition helped me really grow as a person. We went hiking, volunteering (building a classroom) and had some free time. I was a leader for 2 weeks which helped me learn a lot about myself and the way a group works. I also got to see people living in poverty and really develop relationships with them. There are so many ways the trip affected me I can't cover them all!!
- My mother's recent diagnosis of cancer has helped me grow immensely, I have realised how important family is, and not to stress the little things.
- My current partner invited me to a church service. It took a while but that has been the most important event in personal growth.
- Church youth group was hugely formative for me.
- Becoming part of a faith community. Having close relationships with slightly older people
- I'm not sure this is what you wanted here, but the first thing I thought of was the first youth camp I attended. I was going through a lot as a person during that time, but I feel it was at that camp that I grew up, a lot, and there were a lot of (new) people there, supporting me through that 'transition' so to speak.

5. **Which of these areas do you care about?**

- Caring for friends highest, then social justice and the environment
- Volunteering high too (no-one said never for this or environment or social justice)
- Gadgets, games and fashion very low for this age group!
- Social media only 'sometimes'

6. **Who most influenced you to care about one of these issues and how?**

Parents (23) Friends (9) Church (10) Teachers (4)

- Both my parents have positively influenced me for these issues. They taught me how to be caring for friends, the environment and people that are unable to help themselves

- My parents most influenced me. Both my parents were heavily involved in volunteering for charities and were involved in awareness programs for social justice issues when they were my age.

- Caring for my friends has always been an essential part of my life - I don't know how people achieve true happiness if they do not care about their friends and thus probably do not receive the same in return either. In a society in which young people are so vulnerable to mental health issues and pressure from the media and fashion industries, I think it is essential to maintain a real, deep connection with one another and support each other! I think that caring about the environment is crucial in this modern age - we live on this earth and it is therefore crucial to protect it!

- Parents and the community I grew up in; the realisation that not everyone shares an equal and supportive mind-frame.

- My mum and the primary school I went to (a Steiner school) taught me the importance of the environment and animals and all beings in our world. The influence to do as little harm to them as possible is linked to the love and understanding that was instilled in me from a young age by my family, friends and close-knit primary school community.

- My dad, by showing us what putting others first looks like in practice, and that caring for others and our environment is so much more enjoyable, engaging and important than getting the latest and coolest stuff.

- First, my faith. Taking seriously and wrestling with the words of Jesus changed my life. Second, encountering and spending time alongside the poor, marginalised, and disadvantaged. Reflecting on what it meant to follow Jesus in a world filled with brokenness was (and is) both incredibly liberating, and yet challenging.

- My dad, he always had very well thought out opinions on a wide array of topics. I admired that, aspired to have more opinions.
- My parents raised me to be a sympathetic person. They always taught me that caring for others and having respect were important. At the end of the day, it doesn't matter how much money you have or what you do in life as long as you are a good a person nothing else matters (in the big picture)
- Parents raised us with strong values. Strong concern for the struggles of other people and the environment and to practically engage in the political process as well as 'being there' for people less fortunate than ourselves. Always had a very open home.

7. **How important do you think these desires for you were to your parents?**

All very similar – **gratitude** the highest! Financial least.

Financial success is in the sense that they want me to suffer less financial stress than they have undergone (which has been a cause of major problems in their marriage/mental health).

8. **Can you give an example of a way your parents shaped your character to be more caring?**

Empathy:
- By bringing me up in a way that made me see other people and their problems
- I think that the way my parents are so caring has shaped my character to be similar, simply because it is something that I value so much in both of them

Experience:
- My parents took me travelling to less fortunate countries which really changed my view on a lot of things
- Taking the family to do things for others in our community

Modelling:

- They led by example. They would look after us and our pets with care and always had time for us. If we were mean they would 'punish' us and make us understand that that was the wrong thing to do
- Modelled it themselves over a long period of time.
- By example. I think my mother goes the extra mile for a lot of people and that inspired me. I also believe that the love and devotion shown to me has made me more caring.
- I think the best way is by showing care to me and therefore being able to mimic them. However punishment also demonstrated to me that certain things were inconsiderate.
- By being caring themselves.

Generosity:
- One time I was annoyed on my mum's birthday because I was forced to miss the Sea Eagles game to go to a boring play, and my dad made me see that there are more important things in life than what I want.
- Through their own generosity and if I ever acted wrongly in a situation due to not understanding something they would always discuss it.
- By constantly showing me what caring means by constantly giving their energy and time to us.
- An early memory I have is wanting to contribute with my pocket money towards a girl that my family sponsored. I clearly remember feeling like I could contribute to something

9. **What advice would you give future parents who'd like their kids to care about other people and their world?**

Model
- Lead by example. Show your kids love, whilst I would assume we would all (I hope all if not most) would love their kids but really emphasize your love and make it known to them. Be open to talk, don't have them fear they will get in trouble - this is when kids rebel in my experience seeing friends rebel.

- Model it over a long period to show the impact it has
- Lead by example, be inspiring! Make it a part of their world when they are young so that it is ingrained into their way of life.
- Live and lead by example.. no one wants to follow a hypocrite. But to an extent, everyone will be a hypocrite at some stage.. except for Jesus. So........ point your children to Him!
- Overall be a role model to them, display the qualities you wish upon your child because they learn through watching you and your interactions in the world.
- Model compassion, authenticity, and generosity. Practice hospitality. Teach them about the importance of (and responsibility to practice) compassion, both for oneself and others. Don't be over-protective, and don't seek to fully shield them from the pain of the world with excessive comfort. Love them sacrificially and unconditionally.

Listen
- That they need to nurture and be there for their children, and teach them to be caring towards the environment, themselves and other people in their lives; to listen to other people rather than always do the talking, and to show them that although there will be people who have different opinions about you, or what you are passionate about – that's ok, and that this shouldn't influence your sense of self or values. I think this isn't fully achievable if the parents themselves don't set this example.
- Listen to your kids and don't assume that you always know what is best for them. Make sure they value what they have and realise that everyone is different and some people are unable to help themselves

Expose
- Express your understanding or sympathy towards other people's situations in front of your kids, (if it's appropriate) it'll make them see that thinking about the factors in other people's lives is important. Also

maybe don't take your kids side on everything, still support them, but if you express the other side it will show them that they should also consider another person's perspective

- Exposing your kids to things regularly and from an early age is a good way to get them to feel comfortable with diversity and the challenges some people face in life.
- Exposure! Take them to Asia and let them see a world different to their own. Educate them on politics and the issues facing this world! But then bring it back to home and explain how you can be an advocate in your own backyard.
- Try and make an association between yourselves and those less fortunate
- Give your kids love but don't be afraid to let them fail on their own because with everything people need to learn it themselves by experience.
- Be the best example, try to put kids in the shoes of someone else who is less fortunate in some way. And I think people are born with compassion, so nurturing that and educating them about certain things is important.

Limit
- Lead by example having vulnerable people over to the family home for dinner, being generous with money, engaging in political issues, environment etc. Your children will be strongly impacted by the things their parents care about.

Love
- Unconditionally love them, care for them, support and trust them. Have a safe and loving home base is so important for a child to grow and have strong mental health in the future. Allow them to explore the world and have somewhere to always come back to. By allowing them to explore the world they can find their own passions. Role model what caring about other people means. In action! Kids, especially young kids admire

and look up to their parents, parents are the first people they want to be like. Be a good role model. And then let them explore to find their own passions on who/what they care about. If they have been around caring parents and community then it will come naturally because they will know no difference.

- I think a curiosity for other people and the world is a natural instinct, so I think this should be fostered through exploration with other people and the world. Change starts with yourself though, so think about your attitude towards other people and the world before you try and change your children's attitudes.

And Finally

- Always be willing to give your kids the time of day to teach them how to be caring.
- Don't stress the small things, help guide them but let them be their own self
- Encourage your children to grow up. Sit them at the adult table, expect them to be able to take part in conversations and activities and love what you speak.
- Also, always lead by example. If you want your child to care about people and the world, then show them how it's done!

Young Adults Survey (18-30 year-olds)

Q1: Can you give an example of when your parent(s) amazed you or brought you great joy?

Q2: Did any of these issues affect you as a child?
- lack of community
- peer group pressure
- anxiety or depression
- consumerism
- too much technology
- early sexualisation or porn
- poor communication
- self-centredness
- poor self-confidence, lack of belief in your ability to effect change

Q3: Did your parents have any specific ways to deal with any of these issues?

Q4: What's one event that helped you grow as a person?

Q5: Which of these areas do you care about?

- politics
- charity
- the environment
- gadgets or games
- fashion
- social justice
- social media
- other

Q6: Who most influenced you to care about one of these issues and how?

Q7: How important do you think these desires for you were to your parents?

Q8: Can you give an example of a way your parents shaped your character to be more caring?

Q9: What advice would you give future parents who'd like their kids to care about other people and their world?

Endnotes:

Deeper into the Stuff that Matters

Preface

1   Maushart, S. (1999). The mask of motherhood : how becoming a mother changes everything and why we pretend it doesn't. New York: New Press.

2   The Bystander Effect suggests individuals are less likely to offer help to a victim when other people are present. Simplypsychology.org. (2020). Retrieved from: https://www.simply-psychology.org/bystander-effect.html

3   Ro, C. (2019). Dunbar's Number: Why We Can Only Maintain 150 Relationships. Retrieved from: https://www.bbc.com/future/article/20191001-dunbars-number-why-we-can-only-maintain-150-relationships,

Introduction

4   Learn more about The Justice Games at www.thejustice-games.org

Chapter 1

5   Sumner, E. (2016). *Emma Loves Books | The Fairies Of Waterfall Island*. Emma Loves Books. Retrieved from: http://emmalovesbooks.com

6   New York Post. (2018). *Parents Spend An Insane Amount Of Their Lives Worrying About Their Kids*. Retrieved from: https://nypost.com/2018/09/10/parents-spend-an-insane-amount-of-their-lives-worrying-about-their-kids

7   Relationships.org.au. (2020). *What Do Parents Worry About? — Relationships Australia*. Retrieved from: https://www.relation-

ships.org.au/relationship-advice/relationship-advice-sheets/parenting-and-relationships-1/what-do-parents-worry-about

8   I purchased the whole Guiding Children (2019) report at https://shop.barna.com/products/guiding-children

9   Time. (n.d.). *And The Quality Most Parents Want To Teach Their Children Is.* Retrieved from: https://time.com/3393652/pew-research-parenting-americantrends/#:~:text=In%20order%20of%20most%20to,curiosity%2C%20obedience%20and%20religious%20faith.

10   Business Insider. (2020). *Science Says Parents Of Successful Kids Have These 24 Things In Common.* Retrieved from: https://www.businessinsider.com/how-parents-set-their-kids-up-for-success-2016-4?IR=T

11   The Connected Generation. (2019). *The Connected Generation – A Barna Project In Partnership With World Vision.* Retrieved from: https://theconnectedgeneration.com

Chapter 2

12   You can watch a short video training about Locus of Control here: What's your locus of control? (2018). Retrieved from: https://www.youtube.com/watch?v=m95poi3VMEs

13   Grille, R. (2005) *Parenting for a Peaceful World.* Longueville, Sydney.

14   Grille, R. (2008) *Heart to Heart Parenting.* Harper Collins, Sydney.

15   Grille, R. (2008) *Heart to Heart Parenting.* Harper Collins, Sydney. Page 254.

16   Evidence for Learning. (2019). Working with parents to support children's learning, Sydney: Evidence for Learning. Retrieved from: https://evidenceforlearning.org.au/assets/Guidance-Reports/Parental-engagement/Guidance-Report-Working-with-Parents-to-Support-Childrens-Learning-WEB.

17   Student Wellbeing Hub. (2020). Retrieved from: https://studentwellbeinghub.edu.au/educators/framework/

18   Parker, M. (2012). *Ethics 101 Conversations to Have With Your Kids.* Sydney: Jane Curry Publishing.

19   Parker, M. (2012). *Ethics 101 Conversations to Have With Your Kids.* Sydney: Jane Curry Publishing. Page 11

20   Wojcicki, E. (2019). *How to Raise Successful People: Simple Lessons for Radical Results.* HMH Books.

21   Anderson, J. (2019). *The Mother Of Two Silicon Valley CEOs And A College Professor Shares Her Parenting Secrets.* Retrieved from: https://qz.com/1613252/esther-wojcicki-raised-two-tech-ceos-and-a-college-professor-whats-her-secret/

22   Anderson, J. (2019). *The Mother Of Two Silicon Valley CEOs And A College Professor Shares Her Parenting Secrets.* Retrieved from: https://qz.com/1613252/esther-wojcicki-raised-two-tech-ceos-and-a-college-professor-whats-her-secret/

23   Parker, M. (2012). *Ethics 101 Conversations to Have With Your Kids.* Sydney: Jane Curry Publishing. Pages 5-7

24   Paul, A. (2013). *Setting High Expectations Is The Best Recipe For Success.* Retrieved from: Business Insider Australia. https://www.businessinsider.com.au/set-high-expectations-for-yourself-and-others-2013-3?r=US&IR=T Self-fulfilling prophecy or The Pygmalian Effect and the effect of parental expectations about college attendance are described here.

25   Stavros, J.M., & Torres, Cheri. (2018) *Conversations Worth Having: Using appreciative inquiry to fuel productive and meaningful engagement.* Oakland, USA: Berrett-Koehler Publishers. They have a free download toolkit for all areas of life including talking to kids at https://conversationsworthhaving.today/

Part II: On the Road

26   Making Caring Common. (2014). *The Children We Mean To Raise: The Real Messages Adults Are Sending About Values — Making Caring Common.* Retrieved from: https://mcc.gse.harvard.edu/reports/children-mean-raise

27   Barna Group. (n.d.). *Barna Group - Knowledge To Navigate A Changing World.* Retrieved from : https://www.barna.com/

Chapter 3

28   Grille, R. (2008) *Heart to Heart Parenting.* Harper Collins, Sydney. Page 203.

29   Panella., M. (2019) *3 Types of Empathy for a Better Life.* Retrieved from https://maitenpanella.com/3-types-of-empathy/#.X-0SnekzYWo She references work by Paul Elkman and Daniel Goleman (who well known for his work on Emotional Intelligence).

30 Roots of Empathy. (n.d.). Retrieved from: https://rootsofempathy.org/

31 DeSteno., D. (2019). *Research Interests: Can emotions foster virtue?* Retrieved from: https://www.davedesteno.com/research-interests
Read about the various ways he's done this or listen to him talk about his book Emotional Success: The Power of Gratitude, Compassion and Pride here: https://knowledge.wharton.upenn.edu/article/how-compassion-can-make-you-more-successful/

32 Harvard University. (2020). *Making Caring Common* Project. Raising kids who care about others and the common good. Retrieved from: https://mcc.gse.harvard.edu/

33 Ted.com has 10-20 minute talks on every subject under the sun! They are punchy and expert speakers. The whole family could take turns choosing which one to watch next!

34 Brown, B. (2010). *The Power Of Vulnerability*. Retrieved from: https://www.ted.com/talks/brene_brown_the_power_of_vulnerability?referrer=playlist-the_most_popular_talks_of_all

35 Hammond., S. (2016). *Families: Mine Yours Ours.* Author | Podcaster | Parent Educator. Retrieved from: https://www.salliehammond.com.au/ pages 139-166.

36 Worsley., L. (2015). The resilience doughnut: Combining strengths to survive. Retrieved from: https://www.researchgate.net/publication/298718942_The_resilience_doughnut_Combining_strengths_to_survive

37 Worsley., L. (2006) *The Resilience Doughnut*. Sydney: Wild & Woolley. Page 9.

38 Worsley., L. (2006) *The Resilience Doughnut*. Sydney: Wild & Woolley. Page 11.

39 Explanations and resources for using the doughnut can be downloaded from https://www.theresiliencedoughnut.com.au/

Chapter 4

40 Chapman, G., & Campbell, R. (1997). The five love languages of children. Moody Press. Note there is also a book specifically for loving teens and the original for couples. Visit https://www.5lovelanguages.com/ for more info.

41 Bretherton, R. (2019) The Character Course Session Four: Forgiveness. Retrieved from https://www.thecharactercourse. com/session-04-forgiveness

42 Worthington, Prof E., (2021). Your Path to REACH Forgiveness: Become a More Forgiving Person in Less than Two Hours. Retrieved from: https://evworthington.squarespace. com/diy-workbooks

43 https://www.theforgivenessproject.com/

44 Worsley, L. (2006) *The Resilience Doughnut: The Secret of Strong Kids.* Wild & Woolley, Sydney Australia. Pages 4-6.

Chapter 5

45 Piff., P. (2013). Wealth and the inflated self: Class, Entitlement, and Narcissism. *Personality and Social Psychology Bulletin, 40*(1).DOI: https://doi.org/10.1177/0146167213501699; Piff, P., Stancato, D., Cote, S., & Mendoza-Denton, R. (2012). Higher social class predicts increased unethical behaviour, Proceedings of the National Academy of Sciences, 109(11), DOI: 10.1073/pnas.1118373109

46 McCrindle Research and Consumed Campaign. (2019). *Consumed: The State of Australian Consumerism.* Retrieved from https://www.consumed.org.au/consumed-the-state-of-australian-consumerism/

47 Wilkinson, R., & Pickett, K. (2009). The Spirit Level. Why more equal societies almost always do better. Allen Lane, London.

48 Schrecker, T., & Bambra, C. (2015). *How Politics Makes Us Sick: Neoliberal Epidemics.* Palgrave Macmillan.

49 Piff, P. (2013). Does making money make you mean? Retrieved from: https://www.ted.com/talks/paul_piff_does_money_make_you_mean- a good introduction

50 The Commercialization of Childhood (2019) from the Media Education Foundation in the USA. Watch the short trailer Consuming Kids: Retrieved from: https://www.youtube.com/watch?v=8YqWoXeGEt0

51 Moawad, H. (2017) Shopping and the Brain. Accessed from: https://www.neurologylive.com/view/shopping-and-brain

52 Burke, A. (2019). Why kids of rich parents face bigger risks. Retrieved from: https://www.afr.com/life-and-luxury/arts-

and-culture/why-kids-of-rich-parents-face-bigger-risks-20190524-p51qpo - a great article to summarise Biddulph's main ideas.

53   Shuck, J. (2020) *How the Last Recession Changed Charitable Giving*. Retrieved from https://www.plentyconsulting.com/news/how-recession-changed-charitable-giving Note: they have updated this finding post-COVID-19 and are less optimistic today.

54   Luthar, S.S., & Latendresse, S.J. (2005). Children of the Affluent: Challenges to Well-Being, *Current Directions in Psychological Science*,14(1):49-53.

55   Berger, D. (2016). The Privilege Paradox: The Effect of Affluence on the Adolescent Experience. Retrieved from: https://digitalworks.union.edu/theses/272

56   Goodwin, Dr. K. (2016). *Raising Your Child in a Digital World: Finding a healthy balance of time online without techno tantrums and conflict.* Finch Publishers, Australia.

57   Hassan, T. (2019). *Families in the Digital Age.* Hybrid Publishers, Melbourne.

58   DeYoung, K. (2013). *Crazy Busy: A (Mercifully) Short Book about a (Really) Big Problem.* Crossway, Illinois.

59   De Young (2013) Chapter 7: You are letting the screen strangle your soul.

60   Resnick, B. (2019). Have smartphones really destroyed a generation? We don't know. Retrieved from: https://www.vox.com/science-and-health/2019/2/20/18210498/smartphones-tech-social-media-teens-depression-anxiety-research

61   Twenge, J. M. (2017). Have Smartphones Destroyed a Generation? Retrieved from: https://www.theatlantic.com/magazine/archive/2017/09/has-the-smartphone-destroyed-a-generation/534198/

62   Happiness Research Institute. (2019) *Does Social Media really Pose a Threat to Young People's Well-being?* Retrieved from: http://dx.doi.org/10.6027/Nord2019-030

63   Resnick, B. (2019). Have smartphones really destroyed a generation? We don't know. Retrieved from: https://www.vox.com/science-and-health/2019/2/20/18210498/smartphones-tech-social-media-teens-depression-anxiety-research

64 DeYoung, K. (2013) *Crazy Busy: A (Mercifully) Short Book about a (Really) Big Problem.* Crossway, Illinois. Chapter 6, Location 739.

65 Harris, R. (2007). *The Happiness Trap.* Exisle Publishing. Page 202.

66 Monbiot., G. (2020). The horror films got it wrong. This virus has turned us into caring neighbours. Retrieved from: https://www.theguardian.com/commentisfree/2020/mar/31/virus-neighbours-covid-19

67 Harari, Y. N. (2011). *Sapiens.* Penguin Random House.

68 Raworth., K. (2018). *A healthy economy should be designed to thrive, not grow.* Retrieved from: https://www.ted.com/talks/kate_raworth_a_healthy_economy_should_be_designed_to_thrive_not_grow?language=en

69 For example, simplifymagazine.com; storyofstuff.org

70 Piff, P. (2020). *How wealth changes people.* Retrieved from: https://www.youtube.com/watch?v=Pg5QFOuMoN8 This is a great short video that summarises his findings.

71 Goodwin, Dr. K. (2019) *Screen time – how much is too much?* On the podcast Parental as Anything retrieved from https://www.abc.net.au/radio/programs/parental-as-anything-with-maggie-dent/screen-time-how-much-is-too-much/11138188

72 Bretherton, R. (2019) *The Character Course.* Week 8: Curiosity. Retrieved from https://www.thecharactercourse.com/session-08-curioisity (sic)

73 Kashdan, T. (2009). *Curious.* William Morrow & Company. Pages 19-20. Lots more of his interesting info here too: https://www.toddkashdan.com/

74 Robinson., K. (2006) Do schools kill creativity? Retrieved from: https://www.ted.com/talks/sir_ken_robinson_do_schools_kill_creativity?language=en It's fabulous!

75 The Happiness Research Institute & Kingfisher (2019). *The GoodHome Report: What makes a happy home?* Retrieved from https://www.happinessresearchinstitute.com/publications

76 Strieber, W. (2004). *Money Really Doesn't Buy Happiness.* Retrieved from: https://www.unknowncountry.com/headline-news/money-really-doesnt-buy-happiness/

77 Sharp, Dr. T. (n.d.) *Happiness FAQs.* Retrieved from https://www.drhappy.com.au/wp-content/uploads/Happiness-FAQs.pdf

78 https://www.drhappy.com.au/resources/ If you're really keen, some research findings about happiness are at https://www.happinessresearchinstitute.com/publications

Chapter 6

79 Miller, K.D. (2020) *14 Health Benefits of Practising Gratitude According to Science.* Retrieved from https://positivepsychology.com/benefits-of-gratitude/

80 Seligman, Dr. M. (2009) *Three Good Things.* You can watch a one minute video with Dr. Seligman explaining the exercise at https://www.youtube.com/watch?v=ZOGAp9dw8Ac

81 Abey, A & Ford, A. (2007). *How much is enough?* A&B Publishers, Australia. Pages 21-22.

82 Abey, A & Ford, A. (2007). *How much is enough?* A&B Publishers, Australia. Page 30.

83 Abey, A & Ford, A. (2007). *How much is enough?* A&B Publishers, Australia. Page 36-37

84 Grant, A., Grant, G., & Gallate, J. (2012). Who killed creativity? And how to get it back? John Wiley & Sons Inc, New York.

85 Grant, G. (n.d.). Creative Scene Investigation. Retrieved from: https://www.whokilledcreativity.com/authors/gaia-grant/

86 Dweck, C. S. (2008). *Mindset: The New Psychology of Success.* Random House USA Inc.

87 Mintzberg, H. (2015) *The Extraordinary Power of Ordinary Creativity.* Retrieved from https://mintzberg.org/blog/creativity

88 New Zimbabwe, (2020). *Internet Use No Longer a Luxury but a Right.* Retrieved from https://www.newzimbabwe.com/internet-use-no-longer-luxury-but-a-right-minister/?mc_cid=b44fc1049d&mc_eid=20b48923cf

Chapter 7

89 Brooks, D. (2016). *The Road to Character,* Penguin Books Ltd, London.

90   Crabb, L., & Allender, D. B. (1984). *Encouragement: the key to caring*. S. John Bacon Publishers. (I told you it was old!)

91   Crabb, L., & Allender, D. B. (1984). *Encouragement: the key to caring*. S. John Bacon Publishers. Page 34.

92   Harari, Y. N. (2011). *Sapiens*. Penguin Random House. Page 465-466.

93   The Mission. (1986). In Wikipedia, Retrieved from: https://en.wikipedia.org/wiki/The_Mission_(1986_film)

94   Frankl, V. E. (1985). *Man's Search for Meaning*. Washington Square Press,Pocket Books.

95   Kushner, H. (2002). *Who Needs God*. Fireside Books, US.

96   http://www.oecd.org/health/health-at-aglance-19991312.htm

97   Hari, J. (2018). *Lost Connections: Why You're Depressed and How to Find Hope*, Bloomsbury.

98   Walsh, R. (1999). Essential Spirituality: The 7 Central Practices to Awaken Heart and Mind. John Wiley & Sons.

99   VIA, Institute on Character. (n.d.). Bring Your Strengths to Life & Live More Fully
Retrieved from: https://www.viacharacter.org/ Visit for free surveys of your character strengths and explanations of each. You'll become part of their research too!

Chapter 8

100   Thinking together about civil society (2003). Retrieved from: http://www.americanvalues.org This has the Hardwired to Connect research that involved doctors, scientists and youth professionals.

101   VIA, Institute on Character. (n.d.). Bring Your Strengths to Life & Live More Fully
Retrieved from: https://www.viacharacter.org

102   VIA, Institute on Character. (n.d.). Research Points to Two Main Reasons to Focus on Strengths. Retrieved from: https://www.viacharacter.org/topics/articles/research-points-two-main-reasons-focus-strengths

103   https://www.headspace.com/ but there are loads more ... try searching meditation or mindfulness apps

104   George Bernard Shaw, Man and Superman, Act III, "Don Juan in Hell".

Chapter 9

105 Harvard University (2014). Making Caring Common Project, The Children We Mean to Raise: The Real Messages Adults Are Sending About Values. Retrieved from: https://mcc.gse.harvard.edu/reports/children-mean-raise

106 United Nations. (2015). We can end poverty, Millennium development goals and beyond 2015. Retrieved from: https://www.un.org/millenniumgoals/

107 James, O. (2007) *Affluenza.* Ebury Publishing, Australia.

108 Credit Suisse (2020). *Why wealth matters. The Global Wealth Report.* Retrieved from: https://www.credit-suisse.com/about-us/en/reports-research/global-wealth-report.html

Look up your country!

109 United Nations Development Programme. (2020) Human Development Index. Retrieved from: http://hdr.undp.org/en/content/human-development-index-hdi

110 Tearfund. You can have a look or even buy a card here: https://www.usefulgifts.org/

111 Bregman, R. (2020) *Humankind: A Hopeful History.* Bloomsbury, London. Page 12. He's quoting Jodie Jackson 'Publishing the Positive' from constructivejournalism.org (Fall 2106).

112 Rosling, H., Rosling, O., & Rosling Ronnlund, A. (2018). Factfulness: Ten Reasons We're Wrong About the World – and Why Things Are Better Than You Think, Sceptre.
See also Bill Gates review: Why I want to stop talking about the "developing" world
Retrieved from: https://www.gatesnotes.com/Books/Factfulness

113 Rosling, H., Rosling, O., & Rosling Ronnlund, A. (2018). Factfulness: Ten Reasons We're Wrong About the World – and Why Things Are Better Than You Think, Sceptre. Chapter 3, specifically pages 75-92.

114 Wiedmann, T., Lenzen, M., Keyßer, L.T. & Steinberger, J.K. (2020). Scientists' warning on affluence. *Nature Communications,* 11(3107). Retrieved from: https://doi.org/10.1038/s41467-020-16941-y

115 Rozsa, M. (2020). The affluent are consuming the planet to death: study. Retrieved from: https://www.salon.com/2020/06/23/the-affluent-are-consuming-the-planet-to-

death study/?utm_content=buffer28545&utm_medium=social&utm_source=facebook.com&utm_campaign=buffer

116   A great website to calculate what giving away 10% of your (post tax) income could do is https://howrichami.givingwhatwecan.org/how-rich-am-i - compare yourself to the rest of the world!

117   Higgins, S., (2016) *Just Speak*, page 14. It was produced for Transform International. Contact them here: https://transformaid.org/

Chapter 10

118   Sire, J. W. (2009). *The universe next door. A basic worldview catalog.* Intervarsity Press.

119   This idea is adapted from Tearfund Australia's 'Tear Tucker' events run a long time ago but have impacted me ever since!

120   Lombrana, L.M. (2020). Japan Times, TikTok stars and YouTube gamers are the new climate warriors
Retrieved from: https://www.japantimes.co.jp/news/2020/12/10/world/tiktok-youtube-climate-warriors/

121   See www.actforpeace.org.au

122   Ikkos, G., Boardman, J., & Zigmond, T. (2018). Talking liberties: John Rawls's theory of justice and psychiatric practice. *Advances in Psychiatric Treatment, 12*(3), 202-210. doi:10.1192/apt.12.3.202
Retrieved from: https://www.cambridge.org/core/journals/advances-in-psychiatric-treatment/article/talking-liberties-john-rawlss-theory-of-justice-and-psychiatric-practice/BC564F07177A22F5E114E1812E979191

123   Andrews, A. (2016) *The Ultimate Guide to Writing Your Own Personal Mission Statement*
Retrieved from https://www.andyandrews.com/personal-mission-statement/

Unpacking

124   Bregman, R. (2020) *Humankind: A Hopeful History*. Bloomsbury, London. Page 10.

ACKNOWLEDGEMENTS

Writing a book is hard work! I didn't realise how emotionally challenging it would be, and so the support of my friends was crucial to help me keep going when I got stuck or scared.

I was very grateful for my friends who read messy drafts. From the start, Penny Rankin, Kate Ryan and Susan Packard wrote me notes and let me talk through the book, spurring me on. I am grateful to Michael Frost for his very helpful comments and direction that made a crucial difference. Kerry Mawson got my references into shape when I was feeling overwhelmed. Louise Bartlett gave me an incredible amount of last-minute wisdom.

Without Jodie Lea Martire's pages of notes from her editorial assessment I think I would have sunk. Katie Chambers from Beacon Point was amazingly helpful and thorough. Cutting-Edge-Studio saved the day in the final stages and made the book beautiful.

My fabulous friend Jozica Crncec gave me the gift of great chunks of her time and talent to stimulate cover ideas. Penny Rankin's illustrations grace these pages. The generosity of my friends is inspiring and gives me great joy. My daughter-in-law Tanya brought her artistic style to all the visual tasks too.

Jennifer Hayes Yates mentored me almost weekly from across the world, answering endless questions and sending prayers. Jo Hood tracked my progress fortnightly and I valued her prayers too. Cheanne Yu gave me valuable pieces of advice. Anglican Deaconess Ministries gave me a Summer Fellowship in early 2020 that got my research and my confidence going. And Maurice, TJ and Tanya built me a website!

Whenever I felt too insecure to finish, my sister Karen Lee held me up. Karen also checked the conversations. My friends and family's listening, encouragement and belief in me make me able to thrive. Keiran understood the challenges and gave me precious pep talks. Josh's hugs got me through too. And my brother is the best.

I have also been overwhelmed by the generosity of the busy, accomplished people who have spent time reading this book and then offering such kind endorsements.

My greatest gift from God though, is my husband Brian, who has supported my dreams for the last three decades. I am in awe of his generous soul and I'm overwhelmed by his gentle spirit and faithful love. Babe - you've given me a loving family and that's led to everything else I've done of any use to the world.

About the Author

An award-winning and eternal student, Susy Lee majored in psychology and has a master's degree in Peace and Conflict Studies. This helped her consider how parenting and wealth equity play roles in social cohesion. Her eclectic career twirls around the twin themes of social justice and children. It has included state and national consultancy roles with children and families, international aid and development, and advocacy. As an engaging presenter, Susy has lectured at universities and run workshops for parents and families. She lives a bike ride from the beach in Sydney, Australia, dances whenever music plays and has raised two caring sons with her generous husband Brian.